D1303549

A-TO-Z OF

AFRICAN-AMERICAN

HISTORY

OTHER TITLES OF SIMILAR INTEREST FROM
RANDOM HOUSE VALUE PUBLISHING, INC.

AFRICAN-AMERICAN FACTS

A CENTURY OF GREAT AFRICAN-AMERICANS

GREAT AFRICAN-AMERICAN WOMEN

ROOTS: THE SAGA OF AN AMERICAN FAMILY

A-TO-Z OF

AFRICAN-AMERICAN

HISTORY

MICHAEL R. STRICKLAND

With an introduction by Benjamin L. Hooks,
Former Executive Director of the NAACP

GRAMERCY BOOKS

NEW YORK

To Sheldon, Carolyn, Michael, Maria,

and the rest of the Bross family—

for the loyalty and enduring friendship

This 2000 edition is published by Gramercy Books ™,
an imprint of Random House Value Publishing, Inc.
280 Park Avenue, New York, N.Y. 10017.

Gramercy Books™ and design are trademarks of Random House Value Publishing, Inc.

Random House
New York • Toronto • London • Sydney • Auckland
http://www.randomhouse.com/

Printed and bound in the United States of America

Photo credits: Van Vechten Photograph Collection, Library of Congress: 9, 11, 16,
25, 26, 33, 36, 40, 52, 72, 75, 78, 95, 107, 110; Hensey/Liaison Agency: 44;
Terry Ashe/Liaison Agency: 51 Alex Gotfryd: 45; Courtesy Carol M. Highsmith, Inc.: 87

Library of Congress Cataloging–in–Publication Data

Strickland, Michael R.
    A-to-Z of African-American history / Michael R. Strickland.
       p. cm.
    Includes index.
    ISBN 0-517-16300-4
    1.Afro-Americans–History–Encyclopedias. I. Title.
E185 .S893 2000
920'.009296073–dc21
[B]   00-037570

ISBN 0-517-163004

1 3 5 7 9 10 8 6 4 2

FOREWORD

Dear Readers:

It is good to be home. Home is Memphis, Tennessee where I am an adjunct professor in the political science department at the University of Memphis and where I was born the fifth of seven children, in 1925.

From the start of my humble beginnings, I was no stranger to racism and civil rights violations. My parents were hard working people, and my grandmother was the second black woman in the United States to graduate from college. Inspired by their example, I did well in my studies. But my years in college and in the military only served to heighten my awareness of the bigotry in the south.

In 1948, after graduating from DePaul University College of Law in Chicago, I returned to Tennessee to practice law as one of the few black lawyers in Memphis. In 1956 I began my service as a pastor and joined civil rights activist, The Reverend Dr. Martin Luther King, Jr. who was head of the Southern Leadership Conference. As an ordained Baptist minister, I pastored the Middle Baptist Church in Memphis and as a lawyer worked with NAACP sponsored sit-ins and boycotts.

I became by appointment of Governor Frank G. Clement, and was elected to an 8-year term in 1966 thereby becoming the first black criminal court judge in the history of Tennessee. In 1972, I was sponsored by Senator Howard Baker and nominated by President Nixon to serve on the Federal Communications Commission and with my wife Frances moved to Washington. I served as the first black on the commission for 5 years. There my work focused on among other things, minority ownership of television and radio shows and the image of blacks in the mass media. During that period I saw minority employment in broadcasting go up from three percent, and to this day, I continue to work for black involvement in the industry. Today minorities are more than 15%.

In 1977 I was elected Executive Director of the NAACP. I oversaw the organization's positions on affirmative action, federal aid to cities, foreign relations, and a wide range of domestic policies. The NAACP declared formal statements On the important role of the black middle class in the improvement of life in the ghettos. And in 1991 the NAACP under my leadership fought the confirmation of Judge Clarence Thomas to the United States Supreme Court.

Since my retirement in 1993, I have devoted myself to the ministry of the Greater Middle Baptist Church in Memphis. It feels good to return to my home base after full and demanding careers in law, business, government, and civil rights advocacy. I continue to encourage black families to reclaim their family unity and to return to the conventional nuclear family structure with gainfully employed parents who promote strong moral values. I am encouraged that my words in the past have been regarded, but there is still so much work to be done.

Looking back, I see more than 200 years of major changes that have swept across the political, social, economic, ethnic, and racial landscape of the United States. While I am credited with having played a major role in the legacy of nonviolence and political and social reform, my contributions are few among many.

During the last several years, the study of African-American history has enjoyed a new emphasis. Among the latest books to compile the many details of the African-American experience is Michael R. Strickland's *A to Z African-American History*. Strickland, himself is no stranger to embracing his racial roots as an educator and as an author. His work embodies a sincere commitment to sharing and preserving the history and culture of black America.

This book is a comprehensive collection of black people, places, events, and artifacts. Together they compose the story of African-American history. I invite you to participate in an educational experience under the guidance of a devoted teacher and author. As you embark on the alphabetical journey, I trust that this book will serve you well for years to come. I encourage you to consult it regularly and use it to inform, to enlighten, to teach and to inspire.

Peace.

Sincerely,

Benjamin L. Hooks
2000

INTRODUCTION

In the past few decades there has been widespread acknowledgement that African-American history is an integral part of American history. For more than four hundred years, African-Americans from Crispus Attucks to Harriet Tubman to Martin Luther King, Jr. played a role in defining the meaning of freedom. At a meeting of Negroes in New York in 1931, it was declared that "The time must come when the Declaration of Independence will be felt in the heart, as well as uttered from the mouth, and when the rights of al shall be properly acknowledged and appreciated. God hasten that time. This is our home, and this is our country. Beneath its sod lie the bones of our fathers; for it, some of them fought, bled, and died. Here we were born, and here we will die."

The history of the United States cannot be told without including the stories of the abolitionists, the Underground Railroad, the Tuskegee Airmen, the Southern Christian Leadership Council, and many others.

Who was W.E. DuBois? What was the Montgomery Bus Boycott? Why was the Harlem Renaissance a turning point in black history? How did the Civil Rights Act of 1964 change the course for African-Americans? These are just a few of the many questions answered–along with hundreds of others–in this book, packed full of entries that chronicle African-American history from slavery through the Civil Rights Movement to contemporary issues. The entries cover a range of topics that have shaped and transformed black America.

No one volume can possibly contain all the historical information in this ever-changing field. A TO Z OF AFRICAN-AMERICAN HISTORY has been designed to provide the reader with a concise, easy-to-use format of well organized entries about people, places, and events. The book is a valuable addition to every American's bookshelf.

Michael R. Strickland

Ralph Abernathy

Ralph Abernathy was an American Civil Rights leader, born in Linden, Alabama in 1926. He rejected violence in favor of peaceful tactics as a means of gaining political objectives. He was one of the founders of the Southern Christian Leadership Conference and served as Vice President and treasurer. Abernathy helped to organize the Montgomery bus boycott in Montgomery, Alabama in 1955. Following

The Rev. Ralph D. Abernathy (left) and the Rev. Martin Luther King, Jr. during the Montgomery bus boycott.

Martin Luther King, Jr.'s death, Abernathy became president of the SCLC and went on to lead the Poor People's Campaign on Washington, D.C. He withdrew from the SCLC in 1977. Abernathy died in 1990.

Abolitionists

Between 1830 and 1860, abolitionists pleaded for the compulsory freedom of African-American slaves. Abolitionists are credited with having accelerated the demise of slavery in the United States. They unrelentingly demanded that slaves be freed immediately following the end of the Civil War. It is believed that this led to President Lincoln's Emancipation Proclamation.

An abolitionist circular.

Actors

In the mid-twentieth-century African-American actors included Eddie ("Rochester") Anderson, Pearl Bailey, Diahann Carroll, Dorothy Dandridge,

Ossie Davis, Cicely Tyson, Ethel Waters, Ruby Dee, and Sammy Davis Jr. In the 1950s, Academy Award winner Sidney Poitier appeared in genuine dramatic roles not necessarily "black" roles. "Buddy pictures" paired black and white actors, including such stars as Eddie Murphy, Danny Glover, Richard Pryor, and Gregory Hines, who was also a dazzling tap dancer.

By the 1980s other actors were cast in roles that had not been written with a specific color line—for example, Louis Gossett, Jr. in *An Officer and a Gentleman* (1983 Academy Award). Others who have made a major impact include: Laurence Fishburne; Morgan Freeman, Danny Glover, Whoopi Goldberg, Samuel L. Jackson, James Earl Jones, Anna Deveare Smith, Will Smith, Denzel Washington and Billy Dee Williams. They have become some of Hollywood's most critically and commercially successful actors, receiving scores of Academy Awards among them, starring in major films, and working with respected directors. When the original male lead of the hit musical *Phantom of the Opera* left the cast in 1990, his replacement was Robert Guillaume.

Actress Ruby Dee in 1962.

Clara L. Adams-Ender

Brigadier General Clara L. Adams-Ender held the highest position in the more than 40,000-member Army Nurse Corps. In 1967 Adams-Ender became the first woman in the Army to receive the Expert Field Medical Badge. In 1976 she became the first nurse and first woman to be awarded the degree Master of Military Art and Science. Under her tenure as chief, the corps successfully met the challenges of Operation Desert Storm. She later served as the Commanding General, U.S. Army Fort Belvoir, Virginia and Deputy Commanding General, U.S. Army Military District of Washington, until her retirement in August 1993. She received many awards including the Distinguished Service Medal and the Army Commendation Medal.

African-American

African-American is the term often used to name the people who live in the United States but whose ancestors came from geographical regions below the Sahara in Africa. The slaveholder labels of black and negro (Spanish for black) were offensive, so Americans of African descent chose the euphemism "colored" when they were freed. Capitalized, "Negro" became acceptable during the migration to the North for factory jobs. Afro-American was adopted by civil rights activists to underline pride in the ancient homeland. However, "Black," the symbol of power and revolution, proved more popular. All of these terms are still reflected in the names of numerous organizations. In the late 1980s, Jesse Jackson proposed the term African-American.

Blacks heading north from Vicksburg, Mississippi.

African-American Migration to the North

When slavery was abolished in 1865, blacks were an overwhelmingly rural people. In the years that followed, there was a slow but steady migration of blacks to the cities, mainly in the South. Migration to the North was relatively small, with nearly 8 million blacks–about 90 percent of the total black population of the United States–still living in the South in 1900. But between 1910 and 1920, crop damage caused by floods and by insects–mainly the boll weevil–deepened an already severe economic depression in Southern agriculture. Destitute blacks swarmed to the North in 1915 and 1916, as thousands of new jobs opened up in industries supplying goods to Europe, then embroiled in World War I. Between 1910 and 1920, an estimated 500,000 blacks left the South. The blacks who fled from the South soon found that they had not escaped segregation and discrimination. They were confined mainly to overcrowded and dilapidated housing, and they were largely restricted to poorly paid, menial jobs. Again there were antiblack riots, such as that in East St. Louis, Illinois, in 1917. But in the Northern cities the economic and educational opportunities for blacks were immeasurably greater than they had been in the rural South. In addition, they were helped by various organizations, such as the National Urban League, founded in 1910.

African-American Themes in Literature

Many issues affecting blacks as members of a minority community are reflected in the literature about them. For example, the segregation of blacks was evident in books such as *Araminta* (1935) by Eva Knox Evans and the photographic essay *Tobey* (1939) by Stella Sharpe. Racial prejudice was openly discussed for the first time in Jesse Jackson's *Call Me Charley* (1945) and Marguerite de Angeli's *Bright April* (1946). *Two Is a Team* (1945) by the Beims, received considerable attention, since it was one of the first books depicting a black and white child playing together. More recently, black writers have included interracial friendships in their books. In two books by Lucille Clifton, she makes it clear that the black boy is the leader. In *My Friend Jacob* (Clifton, 1980) Jacob is white. His friend Sam is black. Tony Polito in *The Boy Who Didn't Believe in Spring* is also white.

Over the years, several themes have remained constant in African-American literature. Stories about families are highly prevalent. Stories and poems are used to help socialize children toward gaining a sense of pride in themselves, in their families, and in the broader community of African-Americans. Of course, these kinds of stories have a universal quality as well, since the messages and values they contain are shared by many cultures and many groups.

African Methodist Episcopal Church

The African Methodist Episcopal Church was started in 1787 in Philadelphia, Pennsylvania by a group of African-Americans led by the 27-year-old free African-American, Richard Allen. Allen and his group were interested in providing a place of worship that was separate from the church of the white people,

Bethel African Methodist Church in Philadelphia.

providing opportunities that would allow for self-expression and more involvement in church services. The African-American Methodist Episcopal Church originated as a protest against the inhuman treatment which the people of African descent were forced to accept from the white people who were members of the St. George Methodist Church in Philadelphia,

Pennsylvania. Allen initiated night school classes in which people could learn how to help themselves. The church's philosophy of education and self-help emerged from these classes. Bethel A.M.E. Church, which was organized by Allen and his congregants, still stands today at the corner of Sixth and Lombard Streets in Philadelphia, Pennsylvania. Over time, other African-American churches were started in New Jersey, Maryland, Baltimore, Delaware and other places in the country. In 1816, these churches formed the A.M.E. Church, and Richard Allen became its first bishop.

Afrocentricity

Afrocentricity is a term used to describe American and world history from an African viewpoint. Also referred to as Afrocentrism, the school of thought had its beginnings in the 1970s during the rise of black studies programs in American education.

Alvin Ailey

Alvin Ailey was a black American choreographer and dancer who is best known for his use of artistic African themes. Born in Roger, Texas in 1931, he organized his own dance troupe called Alvin Ailey's American Dance Theater. His creations combined modern dance, ballet, jazz, and African ethnic styles. His most famous pieces are "Revelations" and "Cry." He died in 1989, but his dance troupe continued under the direction of his star performer, Judith Jamieson.

Alvin Ailey formed his dance theater in 1959.

Muhammad Ali

Muhammad Ali is the former Cassius Marcellus Clay, Jr. He changed his name after becoming a Black Muslim. Ali was born in Louisville, Kentucky in 1942. He gained notoriety as a boxer and won the Olympic Gold medal in 1960. His poetic demeanor helped to make him a popular figure in and apart from the boxing world.

Ali was awarded the heavyweight crown in 1964 by defeating Sonny Liston, but Ali's championship was taken away when he refused to serve in the armed forces because of his religious convictions. The Supreme Court, however, did uphold his appeal to the draft in 1971.

Ali went on to regain the heavyweight title in a match against George Forman. He later lost it to Leon Spinks in 1978, but won it back for a third time from Spinks before the end of that year. More recently, Ali has been afflicted with Parkinson's Disease.

All Deliberate Speed

All deliberate speed refers to the Supreme Court's ruling ordering the states to go forward with "all deliberate speed" toward school integration. This action took place a year after the Court judged that in "Brown v Board of Education" racial segregation in the public schools was intrinsically unequitable.

Richard Allen

Allen was born a slave in Philadelphia in 1760. He was sold as a child to a farmer in nearby Dover, Delaware. During that time, Allen became a Methodist, and eventually he earned the money to buy his own liberation. Allen traveled throughout the East after the American Revolution. He preached to blacks and whites. By 1784, Allen had become an ordained Methodist minister. Then in 1786, Allen was confronted with racism and discrimination in St.

Richard Allen, first bishop of the AME Church.

George's Church. He left the church, and along with his followers, he concentrated on raising money and building his own church, named Bethel or House of God when it was opened in 1794. It became the African Methodist Episcopal Church in 1816.

Throughout his life, Allen continued to work on social causes. He is known for his efforts to help people who were stricken with yellow fever during the 1792-1793 epidemic in Philadelphia. He also led the first black convention against the movement to colonize Africa with African-Americans. Allen died on March 26, 1831.

American Anti-Slavery Society

The American Anti-Slavery Society was established in 1833 for the expressed purpose of saturating the slave states with abolitionist literature. Members of the society lobbied in Washington, D.C. against slavery.

American Colonization Society

The American Colonization Society was established in 1817 with the primary task of buying land in Africa in order to solve the problem of Negroes in America. Members of the Society believed that they could solve the difficulties between blacks and whites through racial separation. The Society's goal was to transplant freed slaves to Africa, but very few blacks wanted to go. As a result, the Society had little impact.

Amistad Rebellion

The *Amistad* Rebellion is recorded as the most famous shipboard slave rebellion in the history of the United States. On July 1, 1839, a group of Africans were on their way to Cuba on the Spanish ship, the *Amistad*; illegally and against their will. They rose up and killed the captain of the ship. The leader of the rebellion, Joseph Cinque, and his followers took control of the ship off the coast of Cuba. Two crew members promised to take them back to Africa. Changing course, the *Amistad* arrived in the United States where it was captured by the USS *Washington*. In 1841, the Supreme Court of the United States ruled that the Africans were never slaves under international law and should be granted their freedom. Despite their victory in court, only 35 of the original 53 Africans survived to board the ship *Gentleman* that set sail for Africa on November 27, 1841. Arriving in

Sierra Leone in January 1842, almost three years after their capture, these Africans regained their freedom. *Amistad* was the subject of a major motion picture by director Stephen Spielberg, starring Morgan Freeman, Matthew McConaughey, Anthony Hopkins, and Djimon Hounsou.

Amos 'n' Andy

Amos 'n' Andy was a much-derided yet popular American radio and television show that ran from 1951-1954. Syndicated reruns continued until 1966. The show served as an important part of the American minstrel tradition which reinforced stereotypes of black people. The Sam 'n' Henry radio show, as it was first called, was created in 1926 by two white entertainers, Freeman Gosden and Charles Correll. It portrayed its two African-American characters in full racial stereotype, complete with broken English. Together, they were bumbling fools. In 1928 the characters were renamed *Amos 'n' Andy* and were crafted to reflect white stereotypes of African-American life and culture in Harlem, New York. Amos was portrayed as weak and submissive, and Andy was lazy and pretentious. When the National Broadcasting Company (NBC) acquired the radio program in 1929, they became a national comic sensation. Controversy erupted in 1931 when the Pittsburgh Courier, an African- American weekly newspaper, gathered 750,000 signatures calling for the show's cancellation. Despite protests by the National Association for the Advancement of Colored People (NAACP), the television show premiered on Columbia Broadcasting System (CBS) in 1951.

Marian Anderson

In 1939, singer Marian Anderson was the center of controversy when the Daughters of the American Revolution blocked her Washington, D.C. performance at Constitution Hall. First Lady Eleanor Roosevelt resigned from the DAR and arranged for Anderson to sing at the Lincoln Memorial before an audience of 75,000. Anderson made history when she became the first African-American soloist at the Metropolitan Opera House in New York City in 1955.

Marian Anderson singing at the Lincoln Memorial in 1939.

Maya Angelou

After an acting and journalism career, Maya Angelou taught at UCLA and published her autobiography, *I Know Why the Caged Bird Sings*. She has written poetry, plays, screenplays, and earned an Emmy nomination for her performance in Alex Haley's *Roots* in 1977. She read her famous poem, "On the Pulse of the Morning," at Bill Clinton's inauguration in 1993.

The Apollo Theater

With live broadcasts that featured the orchestras of African-American pianists Duke Ellington and Count Basie, the Apollo in central Harlem, New York, was the most important venue in African-American show business from the 1930s through the 1970s. Located at 253 West 125th Street, by the 1950s the theater became a springboard for numerous careers. The theater also hosted landmark performances by artists such as James Brown, Ella Fitzgerald, Sarah Vaughan, and Pearl Bailey. Stevie Wonder and the Jackson Five enjoyed their first major exposure at the Apollo. During the 1970s the Apollo steadily lost money, forcing its closure in 1977. Its declaration as a national historic landmark in 1983 secured the building's survival, but efforts throughout the 1980s to make it a viable performance house largely failed. In 1991 the theater was taken on by a nonprofit organization which had the goal of making the Apollo a significant part of Harlem's 125th Street renewal.

Artists in African-American literature

Visual artists within the tradition of African-American children's literature have made outstanding contributions to children's literature as a whole. Award winning picture book artists include Jerry Pinkney, Ashley Bryan, George Ford, James Ransome, Tom Feelings, Jan Spivey Gilchrist, John Steptoe and Floyd Cooper. Such illustrators help artists see words in specific contexts, and their legacy continues with artists such as Bryan Pinkney, son of Jerry Pinkney, and Javaka Steptoe, son of John Steptoe. Other celebrated illustrators include Pat Cummings, Carole Byard, Cheryl Hannah, and Will Clay.

Arthur Ashe

The first African-American to win a grand slam tennis tournament, he made history when he won the men's singles titles at the 1968 U.S. Open. Ashe continued to win tournaments and in 1975 became the first black to be ranked number one in U.S. tennis. Ashe was active in human rights and political issues, and when he was diagnosed with AIDS in 1992–contracted through a blood transfusion–he became an advocate for government funding for AIDS, going on to establish the Arthur Ashe Foundation. He died in 1993 at the age of 49.

Asiento

Spain and Portugal's asiento system authorized the direct shipment of Africans to designated locations. Payment to the crown was made prior to shipment. The slave owners were promised huge profits.

Atlanta Compromise

The Atlanta Compromise resulted from a speech given by black leader Booker T. Washington in 1895. Washington believed that blacks could better themselves through self-help and self-improvement. He opposed agitation, segregation, human bondage, and racial discrimination. He promoted social and economic advancement for blacks and urged them to focus on acquiring useful skills.

Crispus Attucks

Crispus Attucks was a runaway slave who was slain by the British in the Boston Massacre in 1770. He was one of the first men to sacrifice his life in the fight for Independence and became a hero of the American Revolution. Born in Framingham, Massachusetts, he escaped from slavery and took part in defying the Intolerable Acts. Attucks was the first man killed in Boston Massacre.

Bacaroons

Bacaroons were rows of wooden shacks set up on the African coast. African slaves were housed in these shacks while they awaited their transport to the Americas.

Josephine Baker

Born in St. Louis, Missouri, at age 16, Baker joined a dance troupe and appeared in Broadway musicals, including *Shuffle Along* in 1922 and *Chocolate Dandies* in 1924. In 1925 she became an overnight sensation in Paris in the Revue Negre as a symbol of the Jazz Age. Baker served in the Red Cross in World War II and was an intellignece agent with the Resistance. Josephine Baker married four times and adopted 12 children of different races, whom she referred to as her "Rainbow Tribe." She is most remembered for an extraordinary jungle dance costume made of bananas.

James Baldwin

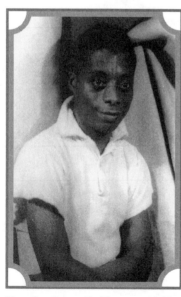

Novelist James Baldwin in 1955.

James Baldwin is the noted African-American author born in 1924 in New York City. His diverse body of work encompasses novels, essays, short stories and plays. Baldwin's well known publications include *Go Tell It On the Mountain* (1953), *Just Above My Head* (1979), and *Notes of a Native Son* (1955).

Banjar

The banjar is a fretted stringed musical instrument that was brought from Africa to America in the eighteenth century. Its chords are the same as the four lower chords of a guitar. It resembles a modern banjo.

Amiri Baraka

Amiri Baraka was born LeRoi Jones in 1934 in Newark, New Jersey. His plays of the 1960s were a significant part of the Black Theater movement. *The Dutchman, The Toilet, and The Slave* are among his better-known pieces that focus on the African-American's hatred for white society. He has also written poetry, essays, and an autobiography.

Bars Fight

Bars Fight" is the earliest documented poem by an African-American. It was handed down orally for over 100 years. This poem by Lucy Terry first appeared in print in 1855.

James Beckwourth

James Beckwourth was born a slave in Virginia in 1787. He eventually ran away from his master in St. Louis and went west. There he worked for the Mountain Fur Company and learned about fur trapping and trading. Beckwourth became involved with the Crow Indians when a Crow mother claimed him as her son. He accepted Crow identity and took a Crow wife. He went on to lead the Crows in many wars with the Blackfeet Indians. Beckwourth is credited with discovering a pass through the Sierra Nevada in 1850. He escorted the first wagon train through this pass that still exists today, north of Nevada. Beckwourth died in 1866.

Mary McLeod Bethune

American educator Mary McLeod Bethune was born in Mayesville, South Carolina, the seventeenth child of former slaves. After graduating from the Moody Bible Institute in Chicago in 1895, she began a career teaching in southern mission schools. In 1904 Bethune founded the Dayton Normal and Industrial School (later known as Bethune-Cookman College) in Daytona, Florida on "faith and a dollar and a half." She then became president of the National Urban League in 1920. After serving as the president of the NAACP from 1924 to 1928, she formed the National Council of Negro Women in 1935. The original meeting place of NCNW in Washington, D.C. is now a national historic site, and Bethune is the only African-American woman to be honored with a memorial site in the nation's capitol.

During Franklin Roosevelt's New Deal, Bethune helped organize the president's "Black Cabinet." She served as Director of Negro Affairs for the National Youth Administration from 1936 to 1944, and as an assistant Secretary of War during World War II. Bethune died in 1955.

Birmingham, Alabama Marches

Organized and led by Martin Luther King, Jr. and other leaders of the Southern Christian Leadership Council, Birmingham, Alabama was the setting for a series of marches in the late 1950s that turned out to be some of the most gruesome events in American history. Birmingham police met the first set of peaceful demonstrators with attack dogs and clubs. One thousand protesters were arrested and a court order was issued forbidding any more protests. King defied the court order and was arrested and placed in solitary confinement. While in jail King wrote his

Mary McLeod Bethune with Eleanor Roosevelt.

famous essay "Letter from a Birmingham Jail," one of the classic protest pieces not only of the Civil Rights Movement but in literary history as well. It became a definitive work in laying out the principles of nonviolent protest. King was released and soon rejoined the protesters. As the enthusiasm of the adult marchers began to falter under the constant opposition of the police and the repeated refusals of the Birmingham businessmen to end their segregation practices, King decided to use children in the demonstrations. This decision proved to be a crucial one, as it created one of the most lasting pictures of the evils of segregation ever recorded. The children were met with the same clubs and dogs that the police had turned on the adults; the police also employed tear gas and high pressure fire-hoses to turn back the protesters. The millions of viewers who saw this on television and the even greater numbers of people who saw pictures of this published in their newspapers were outraged by the brutality being turned against the peaceful people and a national and international cry went up to bring an end to segregation.

President John F. Kennedy, responding to this public outcry, quickly dispatched a representative from the Justice Department to negotiate between the protesters and the Birmingham businessmen. Fearing negative publicity, the Birmingham officials agreed to meet King's major demands, resulting in the desegregation of drinking fountains, restrooms, lunch counters and fitting rooms. They also agreed to more equal hiring practices, which allowed African-Americans to gain employment in positions that had always been closed to them. While the nation, the Kennedy Administration, and the protesters celebrated this victory, white supremacists displayed their anger at the agreement by bombing King's hotel and the home of King's brother. These actions inspired rioting and the Kennedy Administration ordered federal troops into Birmingham to stop the violence so that the agreement would have time to take effect.

Black Aesthetic

Supporters of the Black Arts Movement, which lasted from the early 1960s to the mid 1970s, sought themes that arose from the context of African-American culture. This became known as Black Aesthetic theory, and it generated a remarkable amount of criticism and theory about African-American literature. In 1968 Larry Neal and Amiri Baraka edited *Black Fire: An Anthology of African-American Writing*. In examining how the political values of the Black Power Movement found expression in the aesthetic of African-American artists, Neal and Baraka postulated that black artists' primary responsibility was to speak to the spiritual and cultural needs of black people. Leading theorists of the black aesthetic movement included Houston A. Baker, Jr.; Henry Louis Gates, Jr.; Addison Gayle, Jr., editor of the anthology *The Black Aesthetic* (1971); and Hoyt W. Fuller, editor of the journal *Negro Digest* (which became *Black World* in 1970).

Black Arts Movement

The Black Arts Movement was the first major African-American artistic movement after the Harlem Renaissance. It lasted from the early 1960s through the mid 1970s when the Civil Rights Movement was at its peak, as were new ways of thinking about African-Americans. The Black Arts movement was the literary, cultural, aesthetic, and spiritual wing of the Black Power struggle. Black Arts Movement participants sought to produce works of art that would be meaningful to the black masses.

For the most part, African-American writers during this period were very supportive of separatist politics and black nationalism. Many adherents viewed the artist as an activist responsible for the formation of racially separate publishing houses, theatre troupes, and study groups. The term "Black Arts" is of ancient origin, and had a negative meaning for centuries, similar to "Black Magic." It was first used in a positive sense by Amiri Baraka (formerly LeRoi Jones) a leader of the Black Arts Movement. In 1965 he founded the Black Arts Repertory Theatre in Harlem.

Popular music, including John Coletrane's jazz and James Brown's Rhythm and Blues became important in the Black Arts Movement. Black Arts writing generally used black English vernacular and addressed such issues as racial tension, political awareness, and the relevance of African history and culture to blacks in the United States. Baraka won an Obie Award for *Dutchman* (1964), a play which portrays a shocking symbolic confrontation between blacks and whites.

Rebelling against mainstream society by essentially being anti-white, anti-middle class, and anti-American, participants in the movement were radically opposed to any concept of the artist which alienated him from his community. They moved from the Harlem Renaissance view of art for art's sake to art for politics' sake. Other organizers of the movement include Ishmael Reed, who later dissented with some Black Arts doctrines and became inspired more by Black Magic and spiritual practices of the West Indies.

Another key figure was poet and essayist Haki R. Madhubuti, known as Don L. Lee until 1973. He became one of the movement's most popular writers with the publication of *Think Black* (1967) and *Black Pride* (1968). Madhubuti's collections of poetry such as *Don't Cry, Scream* (1969) used the rhythms of jazz music and language of the streets to reach the masses of African-Americans.

African-American women also played an important role in the movement. Sonia Sanchez was a poet and playwright who brought the female voice, something often overlooked, into the nationalist movement. Her feminism and commitment to black America came out in poetry collections such as *We a BaddDDD People* (1970).

Among the numerous other writers associated with the Black Arts Movement were Obie Award winning dramatist Ed Bullins; playwright Ben Caldwell; and poets Margaret Taylor Burroughs, Jayne Cortez, and Eugene B. Redmond. Other notable writers included Toni Morrison, Ntozake Shange, Alice Walker, and June Jordan. Characterized by an acute self-awareness, the movement produced such autobiographical works as *The Autobiography of Malcolm X* (1965) by Alex Haley, *Soul On Ice* (1968) by Eldridge Cleaver, and *Angela Davis: An Autobiography* (1974).

This era brought wide acclaim to many African-American writers and fostered the growth of Black Studies courses and departments in higher education around the country. It also fostered the inclusion of African-American literature in the curriculum of the elementary, middle and high schools.

Black Codes

The Black Codes were laws imposed by many southern states during the early period of Reconstruction. The codes strictly limited the civil rights of African-Americans, including buying and owning property, marrying, making legal contracts, owning weapons, and voting or holding elective office. These laws also included denial of the right to assembly, job restrictions, and the requirement for special passes for travel. The Black Codes were struck down by the Radical Republicans, but the return of power to the southern states after Reconstruction led to segregation and systematic discrimination until the Civil Rights Movement.

Black English

Black English is the dialect that is spoken by as many as 80-90% of African-Americans in the United States. It was derived from the combining of English vocabulary and African syntax as used by

African slaves. While Black English is grammatically incorrect by English standards, it is consistent with the structural make-up of African languages. Black English is a matter of controversy in American public schools.

Black Fire

The goals of what the editors called the Black Arts Movement were first defined in *Black Fire: An Anthology of African-American Writing* (1968), an important collection of writings in various genres by nearly seventy young African-American writers from 1960s America. African-American poet Amiri Baraka, the former LeRoi Jones, and writer Larry Neal compiled the text. The book helped set the stage for a new African-American aesthetic unattached to Western cultural standards.

Black History Month

African-American historian Carter G. Woodson organized the first celebration of Negro History Week in 1926. It was held during the second week in February in honor of the birthdays of Frederick Douglass and Abraham Lincoln. Woodson was supported by the Association for the Study of Afro-American Life and History. The event grew in popularity, promoted by schools, white as well as black press, and women's clubs. Negro History Week provided an opportunity for lectures, performances, written materials, and photographs of African-American history to reach wide audiences. In the early 1970s, the Association for the Study of Negro Life and History expanded the February celebration, renaming it Black History Month.

Black is Beautiful

The "Black Power" movement of the 1960s was stimulated by the growing pride of black Americans in their African heritage. This pride was symbol-ized most strikingly by the Afro hairstyle and the African garments worn by many young blacks. Black pride was also manifested in student demands for black studies programs, black teachers, and separate facilities, and in an upsurge in African-American culture and creativity. The new slogan–updated from Harlem Renaissance poet Langston Hughes–was "black is beautiful."

Black Nationalism

Black Nationalism is a faction of black militants who advocate the separation of black people from white people. Black Nationalists argue in favor of the establishment of autonomous, self-ruling black communities within the United States.

The Black Panther Party

Founded in Oakland, California by Huey Newton and Bobby Seale in 1966, the Black Panther Party platform demanded full employment, exemption of black men from military service, and an end to police brutality.

The Panthers established patrols in black communities in order to monitor police activities and protect the residents from police brutality. They affirmed the right of blacks to use violence to defend themselves. Their militancy about the rights of black citizens rapidly drew the support of many black residents of Oakland.

The Black Panther Party welcomed alliances with white activists, such as the Students for a Democratic Society (SDS) and later the Weather Underground. They believed that all revolutionaries that wanted to change U.S. society should unite across racial lines. The Black Panther Party grew throughout the late 1960s, and eventually had chapters all around the country. Other influential Panthers included Eldridge Cleaver, a former convict who published a book of essays called *Soul on Ice* (1967), and Stokely Carmichael, the former chairman of the Student Non-Violent Coordinating Committee and a nationally known proponent of Black Power. In the summer of 1968, the SNCC-Panther alliance began to disintegrate for a variety of reasons. As racial tension increased around the country, the Federal Bureau of Investigation blamed the Black Panthers for riots and other incidents of violence. In December 1969, two Chicago leaders of the party, Fred Hampton and Mark Clark, were killed in a police raid. By the end of the decade, 28 Panthers had been killed and many other members were either in jail or had been forced to leave the United States in order to avoid arrest. Cleaver left the United States for exile in Cuba to avoid returning to prison for parole violations.

In the 1970s, the Black Panthers began to emphasize community service. African- American women, who were a majority in the party by the mid-1970s, ran programs providing free breakfasts for children, establishing free medical clinics, helping the homeless find housing, and giving away free clothing and food. By then most of the party's original leaders had left or had been expelled from the group, and by the end of the 1970s the Black Panthers were no longer a political force.

A 1967 pamphlet.

Black Power

Black Power was a term used to symbolize a movement by black Americans whose interest was to draw attention to racial pride and social justice. Black political and cultural institutions grew out of the movement. The slogan of "black power" became popular in the late 1960s. It was first used by Stokely Carmichael in June 1966 during a civil rights march in Mississippi. However, the concept of black power predated the slogan. Essentially, it refers to all the attempts by American blacks to increase their political and economic power. Among the outstanding modern advocates of black power was Malcolm X, who rose to national prominence in the early 1960s as a minister in the Nation of Islam, or Black Muslim movement.

Black Theater

Black Theater is the term used to name the dramatic genre of the militant 1960s in the United States. The focus of Black Theater was the development and expression of a unique black aesthetic. It dealt exclusively with the black experience. Black Theater is marked by the works of playwrights such as Amiri Baraka (Le Roi Jones), Charles Gordon, and Ed Bullins. The plays in this genre are often statements of racial pride and a black identity.

Eubie Blake

Eubie Blake was born James Hubert Blake in 1883. He was a notable composer and pianist until his death in 1983. His musical contributions ranged from ragtime to jazz. Blake is recognized for his collaborations with Noble Sissle. Together they produced African-American musicals such as the well-known *Shuffle Along* in 1921. His songs "Memories of You," and "I'm Just Wild About Harry" were popular standards.

Arna Bontemps

Arnauld Wendell Bontemps, born in 1902 in Alexandria, Louisiania, was one of the key figures of the Harlem Renaissance. Bontemps' family moved to California when he was a child and he attended public schools and graduated at the age of 17 from Pacific Union College (UCLA). Bontemps received a librarian degree and served as the librarian at Fisk University. Many consider his work as a librarian and an anthologist to be as important a contribution to African-American literature as his original writings.

Bontemps is known for stressing a deep sense of pride in African-American heritage in his poetry, novels, and children's books. In 1996, an adaptation of his 1933 short story, "A Summer Tragedy," called *A Tuesday Morning Ride*, won an Academy Award nomination for short film. He also wrote the play, St. Louis Woman with Countee Cullen, which was appeared in 1946. Bontemps wrote more than 25 books, including *Black Thunder*, *Drums at Dusk*, *Popo and Fifina*, and *Story of the Negro*. He died in 1973.

Boycott

A boycott is a form of protest, coercion or intimidation. It is a group of people who band together and abstain from using, buying and/or dealing with a product or situation for the purpose of exercising control. The most famous African-American boycotts include:

Montgomery Bus Boycott: A year-long protest in Montgomery, Alabama, that strengthened and unified the American Civil Rights Movement. The boycott also led to a 1956 decision by the Supreme Court of the United States that declared segregated seating on buses unconstitutional.

Tuskegee Boycott: African-Americans in Tuskegee, Alabama, utilized their economic power effectively when they boycotted white-owned businesses for over a year in protest of a 1957 de facto reduction in their voting power. The boycott greatly benefited African-American-owned businesses.

Boycott in Atlanta: In 1960, African-American college students organized a boycott of Rich's Department Store in Atlanta, Georgia, in spite of opposition from older leaders of the African-American community, who favored more moderate tactics.

Overflow crowd spilled into surrounding streets at mass meeting on first night of Montgomery boycott.

Tom Bradley

Bradley was the first African-American elected to the Los Angeles City Council (1963-71). In 1973–in a landslide victory–he became the first African-American to head a predominantly white city. Called "Teflon mayor," for his ability to bounce back from difficulties without them "sticking," Bradley was reelected for an unprecedented fifth term in 1989. He won a Spingarn Medal in 1984.

Carol Mosely Braun

Carol Mosely Braun, a lawyer from Chicago who had served in the Illinois State Legislature for 11 years, was elected to represent the state of Illinois in November 1992. She was the first black woman to be elected to the United States Senate.

Edward W. Brooke

Brooke was the first black U.S. senator in the twentieth century. He represented Massachusetts from 1967 to 1979.

Brotherhood of Sleeping Car Porters

The Brotherhood of Sleeping Car porters was founded on August 2, 1925, and A. Philip Randolph became its first president. Randolph was himself a porter, railroad waiter, and an elevator operator. The union was for Black Pullman railroad car attendants who worked for the Pullman Company, which at the time was one of the most powerful business in the United States. The union is historic in that it was first controlled by blacks and represented the black porters who were hired as the practice of slavery came to an end. The poor working conditions at the company caused the workers to unite. The union wrestled with Pullman for 12 years before negotiating a contract.

John Brown

John Brown, a leader in the Abolitionist Movement, led the slaughter of five pro-slavery men in 1856. In 1859 he and 21 supporters conspired and carried out a

plan to liberate southern slaves by capturing the U.S. arsenal at Harper's Ferry, Virginia. Robert E. Lee overtook him and his followers. John Brown was hanged on December 2, 1859.

Ronald H. Brown

Brown, who had worked for Jesse Jackson's unsuccessful presidential bid in 1988, was named chairman of the Democratic Party in 1989. In 1993, President Bill Clinton appointed him Secretary of Commerce. Brown died in a plane crash in 1996 on a commerce mission in the war-torn Balkans.

Brown v Board of Education of Topeka, Kansas

On May 17, 1954, in the case of Brown v the Board of Education of Topeka, the Supreme Court ended federally sanctioned racial segregation in public schools by ruling unanimously that separate educational facilities are inherently unequal. A groundbreaking case, Brown not only began the process of overturning Plessy v Ferguson (1896), which had declared "separate but equal" public facilities constitutional, but also provided the legal foundation of the Civil Rights Movement of the 1960s. Brown was a revolutionary decision, but it was also the culmination of a long series of changes both in the court and in the strategies of integration's most powerful legal champion, the National Association for the Advancement of Colored People (NAACP). Pushing the court to this point had taken the NAACP more than 40 years. Since its founding in 1909, the organization had challenged legalized racial inequality. Among the evidence NAACP lawyers presented was that of academic experts like social psychologist Kenneth B. Clark, whose work with children demonstrated the damaging psychological effects of segregation. The NAACP successfully argued three points: (1) states had no valid reason to impose segregation, (2) racial separation, no matter how equal the facilities, caused psychological damage to black children, and (3) restrictions or distinctions based upon race or color violated the equal protection clause of the fourteenth Amendment.

Despite victory, desegregation was not immediate, easy, or complete. White crowds threw rocks at African-American grade-schoolers in Little Rock, Arkansas, in 1957, and Alabama governor George Wallace blocked the door when the first African-American students attempted to enter the state university in 1962. Throughout the 1960s and 1970s, urban schools increasingly experienced de facto segregation as middle-class whites fled to the suburbs. New strategies to achieve integration, such as busing, sparked renewed frustration, anger, and resentment on all sides. At present, many urban American schools are nearly all-black, while many suburban schools are all-white. Some African-American urban schools are

as unequal as those before Brown. The case, considered by many legal scholars to be the most significant of the twentieth century, brought racial integration to thousands of American schools.

Students being escorted into Central High School in Little Rock, Arkansas.

The Brownsville Riot

The Brownsville Riot in Texas on August 13, 1906 began with the shooting of a police officer and a bartender in the town. The 25th Colored Infantry was stationed in nearby Fort Brown, and the townspeople wanted to hold a black member of the 25th responsible (even though a roll call proved that no one from the infantry was missing). When the black troops went into town that night, a confrontation resulted in the death of one citizen and the wounding of another. The African-American soldiers were blamed, and President Theodore Roosevelt discharged the troops without military honor. He also prohibited the soldiers from holding future civil and military service.

Historian John Weaver wrote about the incident years later. He proved and stated in *The Brownsville Raid*, published in 1970, that a black soldier was not accountable. The original dishonorable discharge was repealed in 1972.

Blanche Kelso Bruce

The son of slave mother and white planter father, Bruce held many government positions before being appointed to the U.S. Senate representing Mississippi during the Reconstruction period. He was register of the U.S. Treasury 1881-85, and from 1895-98.

Buffalo Soldiers

The black horseback cavalry and foot regiments of the United States Army operated in action in the West from 1862-1896, fighting among the Indians on the frontier. The Indians aptly named these soldiers the Buffalo Soldiers.

Ralph Johnson Bunche

Born in 1904 in Detroit, Michigan, Bunche became the first African-American to become a division head in the United States Department of State. He was only forty-one years old. A year later he became the Director of the Trusteeship Division of the United Nations. In 1950, Bunche received the Nobel Peace prize for his efforts as the principal secretary of the United Nations Political Commission. He later served as Undersecretary General for Special Political Affairs until his death in 1971.

Ralph Bunche in 1951.

Nannie Helen Burroughs

A leader in the National Baptist Convention, Burroughs is known for her efforts to bring recognition to the contributions of black women in organized African-American religious groups. She designated a Sunday in 1906 as Women's Day. On that day, women all around the country were given the privilege to speak and direct services at Baptist churches. For years to come, Women's Day guaranteed that women would have a voice at least one day of each year. Women's Day gave credence to the importance of women in the black church.

George Washington Carver

George Washington Carver is best known as the African-American who derived over 300 products from the peanut during extensive research as an agricultural chemist and experimenter. Born in 1864 in Diamond, Missouri to slave parents, he left Missouri when he was about ten years old and settled in Kansas. Carver attended Simpson College in Iowa and went on to earn a master's degree in science from Iowa State Agricultural College. In 1896, he became the head of the Department of Agriculture at Tuskegee Institute in Alabama. Carver created many products from the sweet potato and the soybean, as well. His lectures focused on helping poor southern farmers. Carver died in 1943.

George Washington Carver working in his laboratory in the 1940s.

Ray Charles

By age seven Charles was completely blind. At St. Augustine (Fla.) School for the Blind he learned how to play the piano and clarinet and to memorize music. Orphaned at 15, he traveled through the South with small bands. Charles taught himself to arrange and compose songs by singing the parts for another musician to write down. His style synthesizes rhythm and blues and gospel with jazz, pop, and country music. Charles launched a successful recording career in the 1950s.

Children's Literature

Children's literature depicting blacks has existed for well over 150 years. Until the mid- 1900s, however, most of that literature was highly stereotypical—the bandana-wearing fat mammy and the kinky-haired, thick-lipped "funny" boy.

Two early pioneers among African-American writers were Langston Hughes and Arna Bontemps, who received critical acclaim for their combined and separate efforts. They collaborated on *Popo and Fifina: Children of Haiti* (1932), which was subsequently published in several languages. Bontemps received a Newberry Honor Medal in 1949 for *Story of the Negro*. The work of Langston Hughes continues to be republished and enjoyed. *The Dreamkeeper and Other Poems* (1932; 1994), *The Block* (1995) and *Black Misery* (1969; 1994) were republished with new illustrations.

Of five thousand children's books published from 1962-1964 only 349, or 7 percent, included any black characters, and of this 7 percent almost 60 percent were set outside the United States or before World War II. During the time of the Civil Rights Movement, trade as well as textbook publishers began to publish more books by and about African-Americans. During the 1960s, a new breed of black authors emerged who began to capture the complexity and diversity within the African-American community. Among the most prominent were Virginia Hamilton, Mildred Taylor, Walter Dean Myers, Eloise Greenfield, Lucille Clifton, Tom Feelings, and John Steptoe. These writers pointed the way for others such as

Langston Hughes in 1936, during the Harlem Renaissance.

Sharon Bell Mathis, Alice Childress, Rosa Guy, James Haskins, Patricia Mickissack, June Jordan and even more recent writers such as Angela Johnson, Christopher Cutis, Irene Smalls, Belinda Rochelle, Faith Ringgold, and Gloria and Brian Pinkney. The 1980s saw a steady decline. Estimates for the 1990s differ some but not a great deal. Currently about 5,000 children's books are published annually but only about 2 percent (about 100 books) contain people of color. Even though the percentages are small, there are more books that reflect African-American heritage than any other cultural group.

Christie

Christie was the first nonwhite Barbie. After decades of Topsy dolls and Aunt Jemima, she appeared in 1968. There are now many black dolls, ranging from Barbie to baby dolls.

Civil Disobedience

Civil Disobedience is a form of passive resistance to law or authority in an effort to bring about change in governmental policy or legislation. It is often tied to an act of conscience. In the United States, civil disobedience is associated with the non-violent protests of Dr. Martin Luther King, Jr. and his followers.

Civil Rights Act of 1964

President Lyndon Baines Johnson signed the Civil Rights Act of 1964, giving federal law enforcement agencies the power to prevent racial discrimination in employment, voting, and the use of public facilities.

Civil Rights Act of 1968

The Civil Rights Act of 1968 prohibited discrimination in housing. It also made it illegal to cross a state line for the purpose of instigating a riot.

Civil Rights Act of 1991

The Civil Rights Act of 1991, signed by President George Bush on November 21, 1991, made it easier for black victims of discrimination to sue for compensation. It included legal corrections for sexual harassment in the workplace as brought about in the case against Supreme Court Justice Clarence Thomas by Anita Hill. The Act also allowed employees to make retroactive claims of discrimination.

The Civil Rights Movement

At the end of World War II, black Americans were poised to make far-reaching demands to end racism. They were unwilling to give up the minimal gains that had been made during the war. The campaign for black rights went forward in the 1940s and 1950s in persistent and deliberate steps. In the courts, the NAACP successfully attacked racially restrictive covenants in housing, segregation in interstate transportation, and discrimination in public recreational facilities. In 1954 the United States Supreme Court issued one of its most significant rulings. In the case Brown v. Board of Education of Topeka (Kan.), the court overturned the "separate but equal" ruling of 1896 and outlawed segregation in the nation's school systems. White citizens' councils in the South fought back with legal maneuvers, economic pressure, and even violence. Rioting by white mobs temporarily closed Central High School in Little Rock, Arkansas when nine black students were admitted to it in 1957. Direct nonviolent action by blacks achieved its first major success in the Montgomery, Alabama bus boycott of 1955-56, led by the Rev. Martin Luther King, Jr. This protest was prompted by the quiet but defiant act of a black woman, Rosa Parks, who refused to give up her bus seat to a white passenger on Dec. 1, 1955. Resistance to black demands for the desegregation of Montgomery's buses was finally overcome when the Supreme Court ruled in November 1956 that the segregation of public transportation facilities was unconstitutional. To coordinate further civil rights action, the Southern Christian Leadership Conference was established in 1957 under King's leadership.

Within 15 years after the Supreme Court outlawed all-white primary elections in 1944, the registered black electorate in the South increased more than five-fold, reaching 1,250,000 in 1958. The Civil Rights Act of 1957, the first federal civil rights legislation to be passed since 1875, authorized the federal government to take legal measures to prevent a citizen from being denied voting rights.

Beginning in February 1960 in Greensboro, North Carolina, student sit-ins forced the desegregation of lunch counters in drug and variety stores throughout the South. In April 1960 leaders of the sit-in movement organized the Student Nonviolent Coordinating Committee (SNCC). In the spring of 1961, "freedom rides" to defy segregation on interstate buses in Alabama and Mississippi were organized by the Congress of Racial Equality (CORE), under its national director, James Farmer. The NAACP, SCLC, SNCC, and CORE cooperated on a number of local projects, such as the drive to register black voters in Mississippi, launched in 1961. In

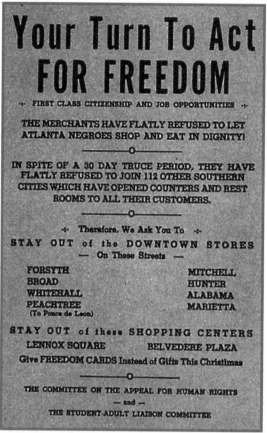

April 1964 they worked together to help found the Mississippi Freedom Democratic party, which later that year challenged the seating of an all-white Mississippi delegation at the Democratic National Convention in Atlantic City, New Jersey. Blacks adopted "Freedom Now" as their slogan to recognize the Emancipation Proclamation centennial in 1963.

National attention in the spring of 1963 was focused on Birmingham, Alabama, where King was leading a civil rights drive. The Birmingham authorities used dogs and fire hoses to quell civil rights demonstrators, and there were mass arrests. In September 1963 a bomb thrown into a Birmingham church killed four black girls. Civil rights activities in 1963 culminated in a March on Washington organized by A. Philip Randolph and civil rights activist Bayard Rustin. King addressed the huge throng of 250,000 demonstrators. The march helped secure the passage of the Civil

Rights Act of 1964, which forbade discrimination in voting, public accommodations, and employment and permitted the attorney general of the United States to deny federal funds to local agencies that practiced discrimination. Efforts to increase the black vote were also helped by the ratification in 1964 of the Twenty-fourth Amendment to the Constitution, which banned the poll tax. The difficulties in registering black voters in the South were dramatized in 1965 by events in Selma, Alabama. Civil rights demonstrators there were attacked by police who used tear gas, whips, and clubs. Thousands of demonstrators were arrested. As a result, however, their cause won national sympathy and support. Led by King and by John Lewis of SNCC, some 40,000 protesters from all over the nation marched from Selma to Montgomery, the Alabama state capital. Congress then passed the Voting Rights Act of 1965, which eliminated all discriminatory qualifying tests for voter registrants and provided for the appointment of federal registrars.

Civil War

After Abraham Lincoln was elected president in 1860 on the antislavery platform of the new Republican party, the Southern states seceded from the Union and formed the Confederacy. But preservation of the Union, not the abolition of slavery, was the initial objective of President Lincoln. Lincoln believed in gradual emancipation, with the federal government compensating the slaveholders for the loss of their "property."

The Civil War between the Union north and Confederate South began in 1861. But in September

1862 Lincoln issued the Emancipation Proclamation, declaring that all slaves residing in states in rebellion against the United States as of Jan. 1, 1863, were to be free. Thus the Civil War became, in effect, a war to end slavery. The extension of slavery into new territories had been a subject of national political controversy since the Northwest Ordinance of 1787 prohibited slavery in the area now known as the Middle West. But by 1857 all territories were open to slavery. By the end of the 1850s, the North feared complete control of the nation by slaveholding interests and the white South believed that the North was determined to destroy its way of life. Black slaves served as a labor force for the Confederacy, but thousands of these slaves dropped their tools and escaped to the Union lines. By the end of the Civil War more than 186,000 black men were in the Union army. They performed heroically despite discrimination in pay, rations, equipment, assignments, and the relentless hostility of the white Union troops.

Shirley Chisolm

In her forty-year career Shirley Chisolm often remarked that it was more difficult to be a woman than to be black. After a career in preschool and early childhood education, she served as a consultant to the Day Care division of New York City's Bureau of Child Welfare. In 1964, Chisolm was elected to the New York State Assembly and four years later was elected to the U.S. House of Representatives, where she served until her retirement in 1982. In 1972 she was a candidate for the Democratic presidential nomination. She remains active in the NAACP, the National Association of Colored Women, and the League of Women Voters.

Lucille Clifton

Lucille Clifton was born in Depew, New York in 1936. She is renown for her prose and poetry for both children and adults and is distinguished with numerous accolades. In 1999, Ms. Clifton was elected a Chancellor of the Academy of American Poets and has officiated as Poet Laureate for the State of Maryland. In 1995, *The Terrible Stories* was nominated for the National Book Award. *Good Woman: Poems and a Memoir* 1969-1980 was nominated for the Pulitzer Prize in 1987, and *Two Headed Woman* was a Pulitzer Prize nominee and winner of the University of Massachusetts Press Juniper Prize in 1980. Ms. Clifton received an Emmy Award from the American Academy of Television Arts and Sciences, a Lannan Literary Award, two creative writing fellowships for the National Endowment for the Arts, the Shelley Memorial Award, the YM-YWHA Poetry Center Discovery Award, and the Charity Randall Prize, among others.

She attended Howard University and graduated from the State University College at Fredonia. Ms. Clifton has been a Professor of Humanities at the University of California and St. Mary's College of Maryland.

Coffle

Coffle was a term used for the forked branch or rope that was used to connect a group of African slaves together. The slaves would be led from the interior of the continent to the coast in this manner.

Nat King Cole

Cole was the first black entertainer with a network television series (1956-57). In 1992 his daughter Natalie won a Grammy music award for her recording of a sound-mix duet with her late father of his 1950s hit "Unforgettable."

Colonial Slavery

The concept of chattel slavery was not one that was initially accepted in colonial America. Unlike the Spaniards and Portuguese before them, who imported African slaves to work in their colonies, the British colonists were bent on using European indentured servants to do the work at hand. There is no definitive reason why these early settlers chose not to use slaves, especially during the tobacco boom of the 1620s, but one theory is that because of the high mortality rate, there was limited benefit to purchasing a slave over an indentured servant. Also, since slavery did not exist in England, it was not a concept that would be widely accepted in its British colonies.

Bidding for a slave.

Blacks who were initially brought to America by Dutch and Portuguese slave ships were assumed to be treated as indentured servants. The first 19 Africans who were transported to Jamestown did not come willingly. Regardless of their status in America, they were probably treated much better than the Africans who landed in the West Indies or South America.

By the 1630s, clear distinctions were observed between black and white servants. The length of terms established with black servants was considerably longer than their white counterparts. The eyes of justice were also not blind to the distinction in color. Punishment of blacks was usually much more severe than Colonial whites. In 1641, the Massachusetts colony passed the first laws relative to slavery. Although they were intended to limit the growth of slavery, the end result was a perceived endorsement of slavery.

Congress of Racial Equality (CORE)

The Congress of Racial Equality (CORE) was founded in 1942 as the Committee of Racial Equality by an interracial group of students in Chicago, Illinois. CORE pioneered the nionviolent strategies of sit-ins, jail-ins, and Freedom Rides. The organization was initially co-led by white University of Chicago student George Houser and black student James Farmer. In 1942, CORE began national protests against segregation in public accommodations by organizing sit-ins. Farmer traveled the country with Bayard Rustin and recruited activists. Through sit-ins and picket lines, CORE had some success in integrating Northern public facilities in the 1940s. In April 1947 CORE sent eight white and eight black men into the upper South to test a Supreme Court ruling that declared segregation in interstate travel unconstitutional. CORE gained national attention for this Journey of Reconciliation when four of the riders were arrested in Chapel Hill, North Carolina, and three, including Rustin, were forced to work on a chain gang. In the aftermath of the 1954 Brown v. Board of Education decision, CORE was revived from several years of stagnation and decline. CORE provided the 1955 Montgomery bus boycott in Alabama with its philosophical commitment to nonviolent direct action. CORE provided guidance for action in the aftermath of the 1960 sit-in of four college students at a Greensboro, North Carolina lunch counter, and subsequently became a nationally recognized civil rights organization. The organization offered support in Greensboro and organized sit-ins throughout the South. CORE members then developed the strategy of the jail-in, serving out their sentences for sit-ins rather than paying bail. In May 1961 CORE organized the Freedom Rides—bus trips throughout the South that attempted to desegregate buses and bus stations. Near Birmingham, Alabama, a bus was firebombed and riders were beaten by a white mob. After this event, CORE ended the rides; however, the Student Nonviolent Coordinating Committee (SNCC) resumed the rides in Mississippi. By the end of 1961, CORE had 53 affiliated chapters, and they remained active in Southern civil rights activities for the next several years. CORE participated heavily in President

Kennedy's Voter Education Project (VEP) and also cosponsored the 1963 March on Washington. In 1964 CORE participated in the Mississippi Freedom Summer project; two of the three activists killed that summer in an infamous case, James Chaney and Michael Schwerner, were members of CORE. By 1963 CORE had already shifted attention to segregation in the North and West, where two-thirds of the organization's chapters were located. CORE underwent memebership and ideological shifts during the sixties. In 1968, Roy Innis replaced Farmer as the national director, and Innis soon denied whites active membership in CORE and advocated black separatism. Under Innis's leadership CORE took a conservative turn, lending its support to black capitalism and nationalism. In the 1970s Innis joined Southern whites in promoting separate schools rather than desegregation. Farmer cut his ties to CORE in 1976. In the 1990s CORE chapters engaged in little direct organization, but Innis remained one of the most prominent black conservatives in the United States.

Coretta Scott King Award

The Coretta Scott King Award is an annual award that is presented to authors and illustrators of African heritage whose books contribute to the growth of understanding and appreciation of the "American Dream." The winners are chosen by the seven member national award jury of the Correta Scott King Task Force of the American Library Association's Social Responsibilities Round Table. The award serves as a memorial to the life and endeavors of Dr. Martin Luther King, Jr., and it recognizes Coretta Scott King's strength and determination to further her husband's work.

Bill Cosby

Cosby developed his anecdotal style of stand-up comedy in the early 1960s. In 1966, he teamed with Robert Culp for popular television series *I Spy*, for which he won three Emmy awards. His most enduring series was *Fat Albert and the Cosby Kids*, a

Saturday morning cartoon show that premiered in 1972. After many other series, specials, and films, he created *The Cosby Show*, a sitcom about an African-American upper middle-class family that ran from 1984 to 1992. His books *Fatherhood* (1986), *Love and Marriage* (1989), and *Childhood* (1991) were bestsellers.

The Cotton Club

Harlem's posh nightclub at 656 West 125th Street in New York City was opened in the 1920s by Gopher Gang leader, Owney Madden. The famous supper club earned the reputation as the hottest entertainment spot in Harlem. It featured black stars such as Duke Ellington, Lena Horne, Josephine Baker, Bessie Smith, Fats Waller, Ethel Waters and Cab Calloway. Today the Cotton Club offers authentic southern cuisine and presents live blues, jazz and Gospel performances.

Jim Crow
(or segregation laws)

Jim Crow was the name given to the former laws of Southern states of the U.S. that provided for the separation of black and white people in streetcars, trains, schools, and theaters. Jim Crow is thought to be an old nickname for a black American, popularized in a song.

Countee Cullen

Countee Cullen was one of the most significant poets of the Harlem Renaissance. He molded his identity through his desire to break through the color lines inherent in American society and become respected solely on his merits as a great American poet. In his poem "Heritage," Cullen explores his impressions of African culture and examines the Motherland's strong role in defining and interpreting his experiences in America. This poem addressed the issues surrounding the black community living in a society that was inimical to their existence. Cullen's use of racial themes in his verse was striking at the time. He became a model for the "New Negro:" young, educated, less fundamentalist and messianic in religious orientation, seeking to come together with the whites.

Dance

African-American dance has gradually developed as an intricate blend of beautiful elements from a variety of cultures. It is evident that African-American dance has had a significant influence on social, popular, theater, and concert dance in America. Lester Horton was the founder of the first racially integrated dance company in the United States. After Horton's death in 1953, Alvin Ailey became director of the Lester Horton Dance Theater and began to choreograph his own work. In 1954, Ailey and Carmen de Lavallade danced in Truman Capote's *House of Flowers* on Broadway in New York. In 1958 Ailey founded the Alvin Ailey Dance Theater which debuted at the 92nd Street Y in New York City. He is the choreographer of the 1960 "Revelations," a signature piece of American modern dance. Ailey discovered the talented and gifted Judith Jamieson in 1965. She is best known for her dance in Ailey's solo piece, "Cry." Arthur Mitchell was the founder of the Dance Theater of Harlem in 1969. Mitchell was the first African-American to dance for a company when he joined the New York City Ballet in 1955. Some of the most well known ballets of the Dance Theater of Harlem are "Dougla," based on African-Caribbean art

and history, and "Giselle," a remake of the classic ballet reset in the Creole community of New Orleans. The Harlem Dance Theater is no longer exclusively African-American.

Geoffrey Holder, who made his Broadway debut in 1954, wrote the music, did the choreography, and designed the costumes for "The Prodigal Prince," performed by the Alvin Ailey American Dance Theatre.

Angela Davis

While at the University of San Diego in the late 1960s, Angela Davis helped to found the Black Student Council and the Student Nonviolent Coordinating Committee (SNCC), a major civil rights organization. In 1969 she began her teaching career at UCLA, but was dismissed because of her radical political views. The following year, Davis was accused of helping black activist George Jackson escape from prison, and she spent 16 months in jail before she was acquitted. Davis continues to work on behalf of political prisoners and teaches African-American and feminist studies at the University of Santa Cruz, California.

Sammy Davis, Jr.

One of the world's greatest entertainers was born in New York City in 1925, and by the age of four was appearing in vaudeville shows with his father. He went on to break into Hollywood, performing in nightclubs and touring. During the 1960s Davis became a member of the notorious "Rat Pack," led by Frank Sinatra. During his lifetime Davis performed roles on Broadway, starred in his own network television show, and recorded many hit songs, including "Mr. Bojangles," "What Kind of Fool Am I?" and the top hit "Candy Man." In 1968, the NAACP awarded Sammy Davis its Springarn Medal for his outstanding achievements.

Sammy Davis, Jr. made his debut as the star of *Mr. Wonderful* in 1956.

David Dinkins

In 1989, David Dinkins became the first African-American to be elected the mayor of New York, the largest city in the United States. Dinkins won the general election after a stunning primary defeat of New York City's incumbent mayor. Dinkins began his public career in 1966 in the New York State Assembly and was instrumental in creating the SEEK program, (Search for Education, Elevation and Knowledge), which provides low-income students with grants and assistance. Dinkins served as president of the New York City Board of Elections and City Clerk until was elected President of the Borough of Manhattan. In November 1989 Dinkins was elected Mayor, serving a four-year term. Dinkins currently teaches at the Columbia University School of International and Public Affairs and is a Senior Fellow at the Center for Urban Research and Policy. He also hosts a New York City public affairs radio show call *Dialogue with Dinkins*.

Charles Dislondes

Charles Dislondes was a free mulatto who led a revolt of approximately four to five hundred black slaves on Major Andry's plantation just outside of New Orleans, Louisiana on January 8, 1811. The rebels marched from St. Charles and St. John Parishes, going from plantation to plantation. They were stopped by four hundred militiamen and sixty members of the United States Army. Some of the rebels escaped, but most were captured and executed. The heads of slaves were hung on display on the roadsides along the plantations to deter others from becoming rebellious.

Frederick Douglass

Frederick Douglass stands forth as a shining example of American achievement and ingenuity–a self-made man. Although he was born a slave in Maryland in 1818, he not only bought his own freedom with the money he earned from his publications and public speaking tours but also rose to the highest position an African-American could hold in the United States government. He became one of the most influential African-Americans of the nineteenth century, and throughout his lifetime earned the respect of not only his friends and supporters but of the entire nation

Douglass was born of a slave, Harriet Baily, and an unknown white man; his name was originally Fred-

Frederick Douglass was born a slave in 1818. His achievements throughout his lifetime made him a model of self-advancement.

erick Auld, the last name of the man who owned him. Douglass tried to escape for the first time in 1836, but failed. His master sent him to Baltimore to work in the shipping yards. This setting provided him with a perfect opportunity to escape, and escape he did. In 1838, with the help of some of the money he earned from working in the yards, as well as the assistance of a woman, Anna Murray, who would become his wife, he posed as a free black merchant sailor and boarded a train bound for New York.

Douglass remained free until his death in 1895. He joined the abolitionist movement led by William Lloyd Garrison, beginning his career as a full-time lecturer in 1841 during an anti-slavery meeting in Nantucket. He became an eloquent and powerful speaker, and in many ways was known more in his time as an orator than as the brilliant writer he is known as today.

Although he was not the first slave to publish his story, his *Narrative of the Life of Frederick Douglass, an American Slave, Written By Himself* was the most successful of all slave narratives of the time. He also began his own abolitionist newspaper, *The North Star*. He was not only its editor, but also wrote most of the articles and editorials himself. The 1855 publication of his second autobiography, *My Bondage and My Freedom*, reevaluates his life after fifteen years of being free. African-American writers like Booker T. Washington and W.E.B. DuBois were greatly influenced by Douglass in writing their own biographies, and he serves as a model for heroism, self-advancement and self-liberation and self-reliance even to this day.

Charles R. Drew

Dr. Charles R. Drew earned the distinction of being the first African-American to earn a doctor of science degree. Born in 1904, he became educated at Amherst College and McGill University Medical School. He went to on Columbia University to conduct blood research. Drew's contributions included his work on the preservation of blood plasma and on more modern methods for banking blood. He is credited with the establishment of better of methods for safeguarding donated blood and the establishment of the blood bank at Presbyterian Hospital in August 1939 along with Dr. John Scudder. Drew died in 1950.

W.E.B. DuBois

For more than 50 years William Edward Burghardt Du Bois, a black editor, historian, and sociologist, was a leader of the Civil Rights Movement in the United States. He helped found the National Association for the Advancement of Colored People (NAACP) and was its outstanding spokesman in the first decades of its existence.

Du Bois graduated from Fisk University in 1888 and from Harvard College in 1890. He traveled in Europe and studied at the University of Berlin. In 1895 he received his Ph.D. degree from Harvard. His dissertation, "The Suppression of the African Slave Trade," was published in 1896 as the first volume of the Harvard Historical Studies.

In *The Souls of Black Folk* (1903), Du Bois declared that "the problem of the Twentieth Century is the problem of the color-line." He criticized the famous black educator Booker T. Washington for accepting racial discrimination and minimizing the value of college training for blacks. In his essay "The Talented Tenth" he declared that African-Americans, like all races, were going to be saved by their exceptional men. The split between Washington and Du Bois reflected a bitter division of opinion among African-American leaders. In 1905, at Niagara Falls, Canada, Du Bois joined the more militant leaders to demand equal voting rights and educational opportunities for blacks and an end to racial discrimination. But the Niagara Movement declined within a few years. He then helped form the NAACP in 1910, and edited its journal, the *Crisis*. When NAACP officials criticized his call for a separate African-American economy, Du Bois resigned as editor in 1934. Although he clashed with Marcus Garvey, the leader of a "back to Africa" movement, and attacked his scheme for an African empire, he lauded Garvey's racial pride. In his later years Du Bois came to believe that the United States could not solve its racial problems and that the only world power opposed to racial discrimination was the Soviet Union. He was awarded the Communist-sponsored International Peace prize in 1952 and the Soviet Lenin Peace prize in 1958. Du Bois joined the Communist party of the United States in 1961 and emigrated to Ghana, where he became a citizen, in 1963. He died there in 1963.

W. E. B. DuBois in a 1946 portrait.

Paul Laurence Dunbar

Called the "Poet of His People," Dunbar often wrote in a Southern dialect but craved recognition for works in standard English. A favorable review of his *Majors and Minors* (1895) by William Dean Howells established his national reputation. His other poetry collections include *Lyrics of Lowly Life* (1896), *Lyrics of Love and Laughter* (1903), *Lyrics of Sunshine and Shadow* (1905). Dunbar also wrote short stories and four novels.

Ebonics

Ebonics literally translates as "Black sounds." The term has also been referred to as Pan African Communication Behaviors or African Language System. It is regarded as the unique language stature of some African-American students.

Marian Wright Edelman

In 1963, Edelman became a staff attorney for the NAACP and was the first African-American woman to pass the Mississippi bar. During the 1964 Freedom Summer project (when she endured fire-hose assaults, attack dogs, and incarceration) and her 1965 battles for Head Start, Wright was touched by the tremendous hunger, homelessness, and illiteracy of children. She also observed that local, specific actions seemed ineffectual in responding to these needs. Following a brief stint (1971-1973) as director of the Harvard University Center for Law and Education, she returned to Washington and founded the highly esteemed Children's Defense Fund (CDF). Among her many appointments to prestigious and influential bodies are appointments to the Council on Foreign Relations and to the board of trustees of Spelman College, where she became the first African-American and the second woman to chair the board. Among her writings are two books: *Families in Peril: An Agenda for Social Change* (1987), and *The Measure of Our Success: A Letter to My Children and Yours* (1992).

Ralph Waldo Ellison

Born in Oklahoma City, Oklahoma, on March 1, 1914, Ralph Waldo Ellison was named for the nineteenth-century essayist by his father (an admirer of Emerson). He was embarrassed, yet inspired, by the name. Encounters with poet Langston Hughes and novelist Richard Wright also influenced his decision to be a writer. Love of jazz influenced his avant-garde style. Ellison studied classical music, composition, trumpet, and sculpture. Early stories, such as the experimental "King of the Bingo Game" (1944), concern the struggle for freedom. His only completed novel, *Invisible Man* (1952), took seven years to write. It received the National Book Award for fiction in 1953. Ellison taught at several colleges and universities. He died on April 16, 1994, in New York City. Another novel, *Juneteenth*, was published posthumously.

The Emancipation Proclamation

Abraham Lincoln signed the final draft of The Emancipation Proclamation on January 1, 1863. The executive order declared that all slaves would be free if they resided in those states still in rebellion against the United States. The enactment only

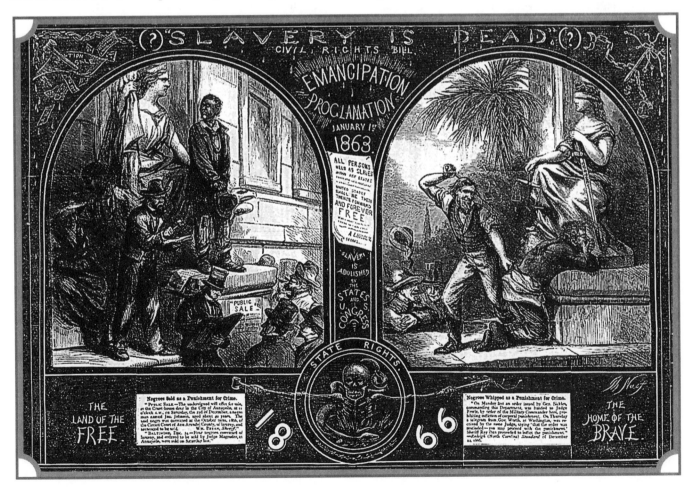

applied to those states which after that date came under the military control of the Union Army. Delaware, Kentucky, Maryland, Missouri, and parts of Virginia and Louisiana that were already occupied by Northern troops were not included. The document was intended to drain the Southern manpower of slaves and to heighten the Union cause in Europe. On September 22, 1863, two major changes to the document were published. This included the omission of the passage that the government would "do no act or acts to repress such persons in any effort that they may make for their actual freedom." The other change was that Lincoln agreed to accept a clause accepting former slaves in the Union Army.

Estevancia

Estevancia was the black explorer of the Americas. He was also known as "little Stephen." He traveled throughout the Southwest in the 1530s and was the first foreigner to discover New Mexico and explore the southwestern United States. Estevancia was born in Morocco around 1500. He left Spain on June 17, 1527 as a slave of Spanish explorer, Andres Dorantes. Black Africans were often known to assist the Spanish and Portuguese during their explorations.

Estevancia and Dorantes joined a Spanish expedition led by Panflio de Narvaez, the Spanish Governor of Florida. Little Stephen was an important member of the exploration team. He easily learned foreign languages and took on the role of negotiator and spokesman. He played an important part in the eight-year quest to find the Spanish settlement in Mexico City. For his success, Little Stephen was compensated with another expedition guided by Father Marcus Niza. This time he traveled northward in search of the Seven Cities of Gold. He reached the Huachuca Mountains and crossed much of southern Arizona. He earned the distinction of being the first non-Native American to travel over what is now the international border and to journey through Arizona and New Mexico. Estevancia was murdered in 1539 when he arrived in the City of Gold by Zuni Indians who were safeguarding their land.

James Farmer

The founder of the Congress of Racial Equality (CORE) in 1942, Farmer was the son of a Methodist minister. He earned a divinity degree and as the national director of CORE, advocated nonviolent pressure, organizing sit-ins to end segregation in public restaurants and on public transportation. In 1963 CORE co-sponsored the March on Washington. President Bill Clinton awarded Farmer the Medal of Freedom in 1998, a year before his death.

Fifteenth Amendment

In 1870, the 15th amendment protected the rights of all citizens against any federal or state encroachment based on race, color, or previous servitude. This amendment guaranteed African-Americans the right to vote.

Fisk University

Since its inception, Fisk University differed significantly from other historically black colleges and universities in its emphasis on liberal arts education rather than vocational training. Fisk was established in Nashville, Tennessee in 1865 by Erastus Milo Cravath and Edward P. Smith, both members of the American Missionary Association, and John Ogden, superintendent of the Tennessee Freedmen's Bureau's Department of Education. Fisk began as an elementary

THE RESULT OF THE FIFTEENTH AMENDMENT.

A celebration of the passage of the Fifteen Amendment.

school to meet the basic educational needs of the newly freed slaves. In August of 1867, Fisk was incorporated as a private, coeducational university providing higher education for men and women of all races. By the 1930s, the Association of American Universities rated Fisk not only as the best predominantly black institution but also as one of the better small private universities in the country. Fisk's art collection and its special library collections on African-American and African diaspora history, including the papers of W. E. B. Du Bois, Amy and Marcus Garvey, and Langston Hughes, are recognized worldwide. Over the years Fisk has had many distinguished graduates including W. E. B. Du Bois, historians John Hope

Franklin and Charles H. Wesley and writers Nikki Giovanni and Frank Yerby. Faculty members have included writers Arna Bontemps, Sterling Brown, Robert Hayden, and James Weldon Johnson and artist Aaron Douglas. Pioneer sociologist Charles S. Johnson became Fisk's first black president in 1947. Booker T. Washington served on Fisk's Board of Directors. Thurgood Marshall, who later became the first African-American Supreme Court justice, was an early participant in Johnson's Race Relations Institute. A survey found that in 1990 approximately one in six practicing African-American physicians, dentists, and lawyers was a Fisk graduate.

Ella Fitzgerald

Bandleader Chick Webb discovered Ella Fitzgerald in an amateur contest in Harlem in 1934. Her recording of "A-Tisket, A-Tasket" in 1938 made her famous. She is also noted for scat (nonsense syllables,

The "First Lady of Song" in 1940.

using the voice as a jazz instrument). Her great vocal range earned her the title "First Lady of Song." From 1956 to 1967 Fitgerald recorded nearly 250 songs for albums celebrating most popular American composers. She died in Beverly Hills, California, on June 15, 1996.

Henry Flipper

Lieutenant Henry Flipper was the first African-American to graduate from West Point in 1877. As a cadet, Flipper endured four years of difficult conditions. The other cadets would not speak to him

because he was a black man. After graduation, Flipper went on to lead a black unit of the tenth Cavalry Indian Fighters.

During his career, Flipper was accused of unbecoming behaviors and embezzlement of funds. He was exonerated for embezzlement, but the charge for misconduct held. As a result, he was dishonorably discharged from the Army and went on to work as a special agent in the Justice Department. He published translations of Spanish and Mexican laws that are still in use. After his death in 1940, it was disclosed that Flipper had been unjustly accused because he was black. Flipper was posthumously given an honorable Army discharge. He was buried in Arlington National Cemetery.

Fourteenth Amendment

In 1868, the 14th amendment defined the meaning of citizenship in America thereby assuring African-Americans who were born in the United States their civil rights. It prohibited the states from violating due process. It gave citizens the right to equal protection of the law.

Frazier Edward Franklin

Franklin taught college in Atlanta and directed the city's School of Social Work until reaction to his article "Pathology of Race Prejudice" forced him to leave. His major works include *The Negro Family in the United States* (1939) and *Black Bourgeoisie* (1951).

John Hope Franklin

Franklin became one of the leading scholars of U.S. history, illuminating the American Civil War era and the American Civil Rights movement. He taught at several prestigious institutions, ending up at Duke, where he was the James B. Duke Professor of History and a professor of legal history at the university's law

Professor of History John Hope Franklin.

school. Although Franklin may be best known to history for helping to shape the legal brief for the landmark Brown v. Board of Education of Topeka Supreme Court decision (1954), his fellow historians revere him for his scholarly contributions. Franklin has presided over several historical organizations, and he has received numerous major honors and awards, including the Medal of Freedom, the highest honor a civilian can be given by a grateful nation, which he received in 1995. In 1997, President Clinton appointed Franklin the chair of the advisory for the Initiative on Race and Reconciliation. A prolific writer, Franklin's most acclaimed text is his *From Slavery to Freedom* (1947; 1994), probably the preeminent textbook on African-American history.

Free Blacks and Abolitionism

During the period of slavery, free blacks made up about one tenth of the entire black population. In 1860 there were almost 500,000 free blacks–half in the South and half in the North. The free black population originated with former indentured servants and their descendants. It was augmented by free black immigrants from the West Indies and by blacks freed by individual slave owners. But free blacks were only technically free. In the South, where they posed a threat to the institution of slavery, they suffered both in law and by custom many of the restrictions imposed on slaves. In the North, free blacks were discriminated against in such rights as voting, property ownership, and freedom of movement, though they had some access to education and could organize. Free blacks also faced the danger of being kidnapped and enslaved. The earliest leaders of the American blacks emerged among the free blacks of the North, particularly those of Philadelphia, Pa., Boston, Mass., and New York. The free blacks of the North established their own institutions–churches, schools, and mutual aid societies. Among other noted free blacks was the astronomer and mathematician Benjamin Banneker.

Free blacks were among the first abolitionists. They included John B. Russwurm and Samuel E. Cornish, who in 1827 founded *Freedom's Journal*, the first Negro newspaper in the United States. Black support also permitted the founding and survival of the Liberator, a journal begun in 1831 by the white abolitionist William Lloyd Garrison. Probably the most celebrated of all Negro journals was the North Star, founded in 1847 by the ex-slave Frederick Douglass, who argued that the antislavery movement must be led by black people. Beginning in 1830, black leaders began meeting regularly in national and state conventions. But they differed on the best strategies to use in the struggle against slavery and discrimination. Some, such as David Walker and Henry Highland Garnet, called on the slaves to revolt and overthrow their masters. Others, such as Russwurm and Paul Cuffe, proposed that a major modern black nation be established in Africa. Supported by the white American Colonization Society, black Americans founded Liberia in West Africa in 1822. Their ideas foreshadowed the development of Pan-African nationalism under the leadership of A.M.E. Bishop Henry M. Turner a half century later. However, most black leaders then and later regarded themselves as Americans and felt that the problems of their people could be solved only by a continuing struggle at home.

Free Soil Party

During 1847-48, the Free Soil Party was formed by the people who opposed the extension of slavery into land that was acquired from Mexico. Martin Van Buren and C.F. Adams were the party's first candidates for President and Vice President respectively in 1848. Die-hard Free Soilers maintained the party until it became incorporated into the Republican Party in 1854.

Freedmen's Bureau

The Freedmen's Bureau, or the United States Bureau of Refugees, Freedmen, and Abandoned Lands, was set up by the Congress of the United States at the end of the Civil War. Its main purpose was to provide aid to over four million recently emancipated African-Americans and over five million whites between 1865 and 1869.

The Bureau set up forty-five hospitals by 1867. It played a vital role in resettling freedmen and assisted others with contract negotiations with employers.

Among its many achievements, the Bureau is hailed for its accomplishment in education. It estab-

The Abraham Lincoln School for Freedmen in New Orleans, established by the Freedmen's Bureau.

lished day and night schools, industrial schools, and secondary schools. It supported institutions of higher learning such as Hampton Institute, and Howard, Fisk, and Atlanta Universities. The Bureau's work came to an end by 1900. By that time, there were over 250,000 African-Americans enrolled in over 4,300 schools.

Freedmen's Hospital

Freedmen's Hospital was established in 1868 in Washington, D.C. The hospital was designed to serve the thousands of African-Americans who went to Washington at the close of the Civil War. Dr. Charles Purvis, the first African-American administrator of a public hospital, administered the three-hundred bed hospital.

Henry Highland Garnet

Garnet was an abolitionist pastor of a Presbyterian church, which soon became a center of anti-slavery activity. In addition to his sermons, he lectured widely and wrote and edited numerous newspaper pieces. In 1848, Garnet published *The Past and Present Condition, and the Destiny, of the Colored Race*, detailing his views on abolition. In 1849, he published David Walker's Appeal, with which he included his 1843 speech. On Lincoln's birthday in 1865, Garnet became the first African-American minister to deliver a sermon in the U.S. Congress. His sermon admonished the representatives to "emancipate, enfranchise, educate . . . every American citizen."

After the Civil War, Garnet helped develop government programs for former slaves. He outspokenly advocated for civil rights, and he championed African and African-Caribbean causes. During his later years, he felt increasingly disillusioned about the treatment of African-Americans in the United States and became interested in emigrating to Africa. In 1881, an appointment as Minister to Liberia offered him a way out. Within two months of his arrival in Liberia, he died and was buried on African soil, as was his wish.

The Garvey Movement

In the face of virulent racism, a "new Negro" developed during the 1920s–the proud, creative product of the American city. The growth of race pride among blacks was greatly stimulated by the black nationalist ideas of Marcus Garvey. Born in Jamaica, he had founded the Universal Negro Improvement Association there in 1914. He came to the United States in 1917 and established a branch of the association in the Harlem district of New York City. By 1919, the association had become the largest mass movement of American blacks in the nation's history, with a membership of several hundred thousand.

Blacks became disillusioned following World War I. The Garvey movement was characterized by colorful pageantry and appeals for the rediscovery of the black African heritage. Its goal was to establish an independent Africa through the return of a revolutionary vanguard of black Americans. Garvey's great attraction among poor blacks was not matched, however, among the black middle class, which resented his flamboyance and his scorn of their leadership. Indeed, one of Garvey's sharpest critics was Du Bois, who shared Garvey's basic goals and organized a series of small but largely ineffectual Pan-African conferences during the 1920s. The Garvey movement declined after Garvey was jailed for mail fraud in 1925 and was deported to Jamaica in 1927.

Whoopie Goldberg

A top entertainer, Whoopie Goldberg was born Caryn Johnson in New York in 1955. After a difficult adolescence that included drug addiction, Goldberg moved to California in 1974 to pursue her dream of an acting career. She worked at odd jobs while performing, and when she began to have a following in 1980, she was signed by director Mike Nichols to do a one-woman show on Broadway. Since then she has been a star, received an Academy Award for her performance in *Ghost*, as well as a Golden Globe Award and Academy Award nomination for her role in *The Color Purple*. She has appeared in many films, on television, and became the first woman to host the Academy Awards in 1994. Goldberg has received the People's Choice Award for Favorite Comedy Movie Actress several times. She has worked to promote humanitarian causes including women's right, AIDS research and drug abuse prevention. Comic Relief has raised millions of dollars to aid homeless people.

The Great Depression

The Great Depression of the 1930s worsened the already bleak economic situation of African-Americans. They suffered from an unemployment rate two to three times that of whites. African-Americans were also the first to be laid off from their jobs. In early public assistance programs they often received substantially less aid than whites. Sometimes African-Americans were even excluded from their soup kitchens. These dire economic straits sparked major political developments. The St. Louis Urban League launched a national "jobs for Negroes" movement by boycotting chain stores that had mostly African-American customers but hired only white employees. Efforts to unify African-Americans led to the founding of the National Negro Congress in 1936 and the Southern Negro Youth Congress in 1937.

Great Society Program

The Civil Rights Movement underwent a marked shift in emphasis after 1970. Legislative goals had largely been achieved. And even more significant than some of the civil rights laws was President

Lyndon Johnson's Great Society program. Established as a War on Poverty, it greatly expanded welfare programs. One goal of the Great Society was to help realize some of the intentions of civil rights legislation. This could only be done by opening up opportunities for blacks in schooling, housing, and the labor force. Thus, a new emphasis emerged: affirmative action programs tried to make up for past wrongs by assuring present opportunities. Sometimes it became necessary to resort to quota systems in school admission and job hiring, a policy that was denounced by some non-blacks as reverse discrimination. Although many black families had risen into the middle and upper middle class by the early 1990s, many blacks were still living in poverty in urban ghettos.

Dick Gregory

Comedian, political activist, and diet guru, Dick Gregory developed comedy routines for Special Service shows while in the Army. He was one of the first comedians to satirize racial differences. Gregory ran for mayor of Chicago in 1966 and for president of the United States (Peace and Freedom Party) in 1968. His albums, include *Dick Gregory, Light Side–Dark Side*. His many books include *From the Back of the Bus* (1964) and *Up from Nigger* (1976).

Florence Griffith-Joyner

Florence Griffith-Joyner won the Olympic Gold Medal in the one-hundred-meter dash, the two-hundred-meter dash, and the four-by-one-hundred-meter relay in the 1988 Seoul Olympics. She also set the world record for the one hundred-meter dash at the United States Olympic Trials, with a time of 10:49. To many, Griffith-Joyner, or Flo Jo, represented the embodiment of a new ideal for American women: a perfect combination of strength and beauty. She had an exemplary record of community service, for which she won the James E. Sullivan Trophy in 1988 and the 1989 Harvard Foundation Award. Griffith-Joyner died of an apparent seizure on September 21, 1998.

Clara Hale

As problems associated with drug abuse exploded in the Harlem community, Clara Hale took action. Within six months, "Mother" Hale had 22 babies of heroin-addicted women in her five-room apartment. In 1969 she founded Hale House, a home for infants addicted before birth. It was the first–and only known program–in the U.S. designed to deal with infants born

Mother Clara Hale in 1985.

addicted to illegal drugs. Through 1975, it was the only African-American licensed voluntary child-care agency in the country. In the 1980s, when AIDS reached epidemic proportions, Hale took on the care of AIDS-infected babies and children. Named the "Mother Teresa of New York," Hale cared for over 500 children at Hale House.

In his 1985 State of the Union Address, President Ronald Reagan called Mother Hale an American hero. In 1987, she was awarded two of the Salvation Army's highest honors. Since Hale's death in 1992, her daughter, Lorraine, who worked side by side with her mother for 25 years, has carried on work of Hale House.

Alex Haley

In 1977, almost two million people watched the television version of Haley's 1976 novel *Roots: The Sage of an American Family*. The son of a professor, Haley served in the U.S. Coast Guard for 20 years until he left to become a

Alex Hayley's bestselling *Roots* has been translated into 26 languages.

freelance writer in 1959. He wrote many articles and in 1965 co-authored the *Autobiography of Malcolm X*. Roots received special citations from the Pulitzer Prize Committee and the National Book Award Committee, and the National Urban League director called the television production of *Roots* "the single most spectacular educational experience in race relations in America." Haley received the NAACP's Spingarn Medal in 1977.

David Hammons

Born in 1943 in Springfield, Illinois Hammons is recognized for his politically provocative and innovative art of African-Americans. His controversial themes have drawn national attention. He has been a fellow at the Academy of Rome and the recipient of a MacArthur Foundation Fellowship and two National Endowments for the Arts Fellowships. Among his well-known works are "Injustice Case" and "How Ya Like Me Now?" which is a sixteen-foot tall portrait of Jesse Jackson as a white man.

Hampton University

A private coeducational institution of higher learning founded during Reconstruction to train African-American teachers, Hampton Normal and Agricultural Institute opened its doors in 1868. In the years following the Emancipation Proclamation in 1863, thousands of African-Americans had settled on the Virginia Peninsula. Samuel Chapman Armstrong, a white brigadier general who commanded black troops during the Civil War, established Hampton to help former slaves achieve self-sufficiency. Under Armstrong's guidance, and with the financial support of Northern philanthropists and religious groups, Hampton developed a system of industrial education that became the model for African-American education. The Hampton Idea emphasized the cultivation of practical skills, moral character, and a strong work ethic. Students were required to spend two days a week working on the school's farm and in trade shops, where they applied their classroom knowledge of botany and arithmetic. Students also received social instruction in Christian morality, personal hygiene, and social etiquette. In 1932 Hampton became an accredited four-year institution and in 1956 it organized a division of graduate studies. In the 1990s, Hampton had an enrollment of more than 5,500 students pursuing degrees in 50 areas of study.

Lorraine Hansberry

In 1958, Hansberry's *A Raisin in the Sun*, produced, directed, and performed by blacks, was the first Broadway play by a black woman. Her childhood in Chicago as the daughter of the founder of one of the city's African-American banks, and the family's failure to move into an all-white neighborhood, served as the inspiration for the play. Adapted as *Raisin*, it won a Tony for best musical in 1974. Her second Broadway play, *The Sign in Sidney Brustein's Window* opened in 1964 and was still running when she died of cancer in 1965 at the age of 34. *To Be Young, Gifted, and Black*, based on her writings, was produced off-Broadway after her death by her husband, Robert Nemiroff.

Harlem

Harlem, part of Manhattan, was originally founded by the Dutch in 1658 and called Nieuw Haarlem. Annexed to New York City in 1731, it remained a rural community until the nineteenth century.

Between 1820 and 1920, agricultural crises in the South, coupled with a labor shortage in the industrial North, led to the migration of approximately two million African-Americans. They came in search of jobs and a better life. Their participation in the urban industrial work force resulted in greater racial cohesiveness and economic independence. This met with resistance from some conservative whites, provoking a revival of the Ku Klux Klan and an outbreak of racial violence.

This period of social conflict and upheaval inspired black intellectuals to reexamine their role in American society and their unique cultural heritage. African-Americans fought in World War I to make the world safe for democracy but returned home to be confronted with racism, unemployment, and poverty. However, their racial identity had been solidified by

their experiences in Europe, which had made African-Americans more aware of this country's prejudices. "The war to end all wars" had made them now more eager than ever to change their condition. After World War I, African-Americans began to fully recognize that there was a major thing that racism and poverty could not take away – their culture. An influx of African-Americans made Harlem one of the largest black settlements in the United States during 1905 through 1920. Harlem then became a social, political, and cultural center for black people in America. After World War II, Harlem fell into economic depression and suffered a high rate of unemployment.

Harlem Boys Choir

Walter Turnbull founded the Boys Choir of Harlem in 1970. Taking a holistic approach to instruction, the choir work includes teaching its young members about life as well as music and sends a large percentage of its alumni to college. It evolved from a small church choir to an internationally acclaimed musical group. They have performed all over the world, and have been featured on the soundtracks of several movies, including *Glory and Malcolm X*. They have also produced an album, titled *A Song of Hope*.

Harlem Globetrotters

Founded as the Savoy Big Five, the Harlem Globetrotters were re-christened by Abe Saperstein, who named them and coached the Globetrotters from 1926 to 1966. In 1927, the Globetrotters played their first game in Hinckley, Illinois. They won the World Championship in 1940 and the International Cup Tournament in Mexico City in 1943. In the mid-1940s, the Globetrotters redefined their style of play to show off their mastery of trick shots, fancy behind-the-back passes, effortlessly evasive dribbling, and other basketball tricks. By the 1950s, demand for the Globetrotters was so great that Saperstein formed a second team to tour the western United States while the original squad remained in the East. As its popularity soared, the team began to live up to its name, touring Europe, North Africa, South America, and the USSR. Two legendary Globetrotters played beginning in the 1950s and 1960s, Meadowlark Lemon and Fred "Curly" Neal. Another former Globetrotter, Wilt Chamberlain went on to become one of the NBA's all-time greats. The Globetrotters continue to amuse audiences in the United States and abroad.

Harlem Renaissance

Two events, the Great Migration and the end of World War I, contributed to the beginning of the Harlem Renaissance. The Harlem Renaissance is generally considered the first significant movement of black writers and artists in the United States.

First called New Negro Movement, the Harlem Renaissance, lasting from 1919 until 1940, was a dramatic upsurge of creativity in African-American literature, music, and art. The celebration of African-American culture came at a time in America's history when the restraints of the Victorian era were giving way to the boldness of the Roaring Twenties. The word renaissance, literally, means rebirth. However, the Harlem Renaissance was actually unprecedented in its variety and scope. Its participants celebrated the uniqueness of African-American poetry, fiction, drama, essay, music, dance, painting, and sculpture. During this period, the first influential African-American literary journals were established, and African-American authors and artists received their first serious critical appraisal and widespread recognition. New and established African-American writers published more fiction and poetry than ever before.

Many young African-American writers came into prominence during the Harlem Renaissance. With both black and white readers eager to experience a slice of African-American life, the literature of the time provided that experience. The most popular and prolific poet of the 1920s was Langston Hughes, whose work delves into the lives of the black working class. Arna Bontemps poems "The Return" and "Golgotha Is a Mountain" won awards given by *Opportunity Magazine*. Another major figure of the period, Countee Cullen, wrote poems exploring the problem of racism and the meaning of Africa for African-Americans. Among fiction writers, Claude McKay stands out as the author

One of the most prolific writers of the Harlem Renaissance was Langston Hughes.

of *Home to Harlem* (1928), the first commercially successful novel by a black writer. Other notable novels of the era include Nella Larsen's *Passing* (1929), which focuses on sophisticated middle class black women who are unable to escape the restrictions of racism; and Jean Toomer's innovative novel *Cane* (1923), which demonstrates a strong identification with poor blacks. Many other authors, including James Weldon Johnson, Zora Neale Hurston, Nella Larson, Rudolph Fisher, Georgia Douglas Johnson, Serling Brown, and Jessie Faussett received recognition. To carve a niche for themselves in the literary scene, young, educated African-Americans traveled to New York City, in particular to Harlem, which was the cultural and artistic center of African-Americans. Something approaching a cultural revolution took place. Black leader, sociologist, and historian W.E.B. DuBois labeled this gathering the Talented Tenth. DuBois envisioned that this ten percent of African-American intellectuals and artists would lead African-Americans in the United States. In Harlem these intellectuals and artists debated about the future of African-Americans. The impulse of artists was to create boldly expressive, high quality art as a response to their social conditions.

The Harlem Renaissance was formally recognized as a movement in 1925 with the publication of Locke's anthology *The New Negro: An Interpretation*, in which he described the "New Negroes" of the 1920s. According to scholar Arnold Rampersad, *The New Negro* is the Harlem Renaissance's "definitive text, its Bible." It offered a definition of the cultural movement. The Harlem Renaissance artists took on the self-appointed challenge to communicate the ills of racism with art rather than argument. They sought to chisel out a unique, African-centered culture for blacks and to simultaneously improve relations with whites.

The Harlem Renaissance writers reflected both the "uplifting" theme of the conservative African-American critics and the "realistic" artist movement of the younger, more radical African-American critics. Both sides succeeded in showing African-Americans and the world that their culture was a worthy literary topic, a theme that would reemerge during the Black Power movement of the mid-1960s and early 1970s. Essayist Eric Walrond, novelist Walter White, folklorist Zora Neale Hurston, novelist Rudolph Fisher, and poet William Waring Cuney are some of the other writers of the Harlem Renaissance.

The Harlem Renaissance also arrived on the American stage, beginning with the Broadway opening of the black musical *Shuffle Along* in 1921. At the same time, jazz was coming into its own in New York City and Chicago. The Great Depression caused many of the artists to leave New York or to take other jobs to tide them over the hard times.

John Henry

John Henry holds a place of distinction in American folklore (not just African-American folklore) as the first and probably only folk hero to battle a machine. While his counterparts like Paul Bunyan, Davy Crockett, and Johnny Appleseed tamed the American landscape, fighting with animals and people who threatened to take over American land, John Henry took on one of the greatest threats to laborers everywhere—technology. A freed slave, John Henry began working on the Big Bend Tunnel through the Alleghenies. It was there that he died "with a hammer in his hand," racing a machine that threatened to take away his work.

Some historians do say that John Henry was a real man—or based on a famous steel-driver named John Hardy—and that there actually was a race that occurred sometime between 1870 and 1872. His legend became a significant icon to both white and black Americans of all ages and occupations, used by railroad workers and union organizers as well as artists. Many plays, novels and short stories by both white and African-American writers have been written about John Henry and he has inspired characters in novels and has been the topic of many poems.

Matthew Henson

Henson, a skilled seaman from Charles County, Maryland was born in 1866, had the reputation of being a well-read adventure seeker. Orphaned as a youth, Henson was 12 when he went to sea as a cabin boy on a sailing ship. While a store clerk in Washington, D.C., met Robert E. Peary and was hired as his valet for a trip to survey canal sites in Nicaragua in 1887-88. Henson next accompanied Peary on many expeditions to the Arctic, beginning in 1891. Henson's resourcefulness with handling equipment made him indispensable to Peary in polar exploration. In the spring of 1909, Peary chose Henson for his last attempt to reach the North Pole. Henson reached the North Pole, or Camp Jessup as it was called, forty-five minutes before Peary. Henson planted the American flag that marked the spot. Congress gave Henson a medal for his work, and upon his death in 1955, he was buried in Arlington Cemetery next to Peary.

Benjamin Hooks

Benjamin Hooks was born the fifth of seven children in Memphis Tennessee on January 31, 1925. He is best known as the former Executive Director of the NAACP from 1977 until his retirement in 1992. Hooks had an illustrious career. He graduated DePaul University in Chicago and went on to practice law in Memphis at a time when there were few black lawyers. He then joined the Reverend Dr. Martin Luther King Jr.'s Southern Leadership Conference and became an ordained Baptist Minister. Hooks participated in NAACP sponsored sit-ins and preached at the Middle Baptist Church in Memphis.

Hooks distinguished himself as the first black criminal court judge in the history of Tennessee and was the first black appointee to the Federal Communications Commission. While with the FCC, Hooks helped to bring about an increase in minority employment in broadcasting. As Executive Director of the NAACP, Hooks is credited with increasing the organization's membership to several hundred thousand people. He prompted the organization's positions on affirmative action, federal aid to cities, foreign relations with repressive governments, the valuable role of the black middle class and the betterment of life in the ghettos. In 1992 Hooks returned to Memphis and devoted himself to the ministry of the Greater Middle Baptist Church in his home state. He works with students in the Memphis City School System and continues his work in civil rights.

Lena Horne

After her film debut in *Panama Hattie* (1942), Horne became the first black artist given a longterm movie contract. In 1943 she starred in the musicals *Cabin in the Sky* and *Stormy Weather*. Horne starred on Broadway in *Jamaica* in 1957-58. In 1981-82 her popular one-woman show, *Lena Horne–The Lady and Her Music*, played on Broadway, then toured the United States and England (1983-84). The show later was featured on television. She won a Spingarn Medal 1983.

Michael Howard

Michael Howard of Mississippi was one of the first African-Americans to become a cadet at West Point in 1870. He did not graduate.

Howard University

Howard University, a historically and predominantly black university located in Washington, D.C., began in 1866 when ten members of the First Congregational Society of Washington, D.C. established the Howard Normal and Theological Institute for Education of Teachers and Preachers. Two months later, the board of trustees shortened its name to Howard University and opened its doors to four young white girls—the daughters of some of the university's trustees and faculty.

Although abolitionist Frederick Douglass was appointed to the university's board in 1871 and educator Booker T. Washington in 1907, very few African-Americans were involved in governance of the university during its early years. In addition, early financial support came from white sources. During the institution's first five years, it received most of its financial support from the Freedmen's Bureau, a federal welfare agency for former slaves. The bureau closed in 1872, and in 1879 the U.S. Congress agreed to make an annual appropriation to the university.

Mordecai Johnson, appointed Howard's first black president in 1926, transformed the university into a major institution of higher learning. When Johnson first arrived at Howard, the university was composed of eight unaccredited schools and colleges, with a total enrollment of 1,700 and a budget of $700,000. At his retirement 34 years later, Howard had ten nationally

Howard University in its early days.

accredited schools and colleges, 6,000 students, and an $8 million budget. The reputation of Howard's faculty grew during this time, when the university included scholars such as biologist Ernest E. Just, historian Kelly Miller, writer Alain Locke, sociologist E. Franklin Frazier, and economist Abram Harris, Jr. In 1960 James M. Nabrit, a leading constitutional lawyer and former dean of the Howard Law School, succeeded Johnson as president. Nabrit is credited with establishing the first systematic civil rights course at an American law school. In the late 1960s, student demonstrators demanded and won an African-American studies department. In 1989 hundreds of student protesters lead by Newark activist Ras Baraka, a Howard student at the time, forced Lee Atwater, chairman of the Republican Party, to resign from the university's board of trustees. Student activists were also successful in forcing the university's financial divestment from South Africa because of its apartheid policies.

Howard's more than 70,000 students have included diplomat Ralph Bunche, surgeon Charles Drew, author Zora Neale Hurston, U.S. Supreme Court Justice Thurgood Marshall, and Nobel laureate Toni Morrison. The university also houses the Moorland-Spingarn Research Collection, one of the most comprehensive black research collections in the world. Howard has the largest concentration of African-American students and faculty of any university in the world.

Langston Hughes

In forty years, Langston Hughes wrote sixteen books of poetry, two novels, three collections of short stories, four volumes of editorial and documentary works, twenty plays, three autobiographies, twelve radio and television scripts, dozens of magazine articles, children's poetry, musicals, and operas.

Born in Joplin, Missouri in 1902 to an abolitionist family, Hughes was the grandson of James Mercer Langston, the first black American to be elected to public office in 1855. He was a graduate of Lincoln University in Pennsylvania in 1929 and later received an honorary LittD. in 1943. He was awarded a Guggenheim Fellowship in 1935 and a Rosenwald Fellowship in 1940. Hughes' first published poem "The Negro Speaks of Riches" is one of his most famous. After 1923, Hughes was strongly influenced by jazz as evidenced in "The Weary Blues."

His work flourished during the Harlem Renaissance in 1924. "The Negro Artist and the Racial Mountain, " an essay he wrote in 1926 appeared in Nation and addressed black writers and poets. Langston Hughes died of cancer on May 22, 1967. His former home at 20 East 127th Street in Harlem, New York, has been given landmark status by the New York City Preservation Commission, and the street has been renamed Langston Hughes Place.

"I Have a Dream" Speech

The famous speech given by Dr. Martin Luther King, Jr. in front of the Lincoln Memorial at the March on Washington–largely improvised as King deviated from the text that he had worked all night trying to write–has been called "the most eloquent of his career." He mesmerized the crowd with his deep, resounding voice, rhythmic repetition of the phrase "I Have a Dream," and the picture he painted of a "promised land" where there was racial equality and equal justice for all. He pointed out that despite the fact that the nation was celebrating the centennial anniversary of Lincoln's Emancipation Proclamation, the children of the freed slaves did not feel emancipated at all, but rather were still fighting for equal rights.

Indentured Servants

The Africans who were first brought to America around 1619, were brought in as indentured servants, bound by contract into the service of an employer for at least seven years. By 1651, several of the original twenty African indentured servants had fulfilled their time of service. They acquired land as part of the arrangement along with their freedom. One such indentured servant, Mr. Anthony Johnson, became a prosperous farmer and master of several white indentured servants. By the end of the seventeenth century, all Africans brought into or born in Virginia were declared slaves.

J

Blyden Jackson

Blyden Jackson was the first black professor who integrated the faculty at the University of North Carolina at Chapel Hill in 1969. He later was the first black professor to receive tenure at the University. During his career, Jackson earned distinction as an early leader in the study of African-American literature as a part of the American literature curriculum. Born in Paducah, Kentucky in 1910, Jackson died at the age of 89 in May, 2000.

Jesse Jackson

Jesse Jackson has become the most visible African-American leader since Martin Luther King, Jr., and even came close to a U.S. presidential nomination. Born in 1941 in Greenville, South Carolina, Jackson became committed to the civil right movement during college and directed the southeastern operation of the Congress for Racial Equality. He became an ordained Baptist minister and in 1965 joined King's SCLC. After King's assassination in 1968, Jackson formed People United to Save Humanity (PUSH), which focused on promoting black economic progress and political participation. Entering politics in the 1980s, his Rainbow Coalition won 7 million of 23 million votes cast in state primaries. In 1993, Jesse Jackson was awarded the Martin Luther King, Jr. Nonviolent Peace Prize and during the Kosovo crisis in 1999 he received a commendation from the U.S. Senate for winning the release of three American soldiers captured in Yugoslavia.

The Reverend Jesse Jackson.

Michael Jackson

Born in Gary, Indiana in 1958, by the time Michael Jackson was six he was performing with four of his brothers and by 1969 the Jackson Five had signed a contract with Motown Records. During their years at Motown, the group recorded 13 consecutive hits. As an adult, Michael had his own contract with Motown and became a star. During the 1980s, Michael Jackson had the largest following of any African-American singer in the history of popular music. The album *Thriller*, sold 40 million copies around the world.

Jamestown

The first permanent British settlement in North America was founded in Jamestown, Virginia in 1607. Twelve years later, twenty Africans arrived on the Atlantic shores to work as indentured servants. Their tenure ranged from four to seven years before receiving their freedom. The concept of permanent enslavement in the British colonies would not come until forty-one years later when the Virginia colony enacted laws of permanent forced servitude. The other colonies soon followed their lead, as blacks became the property of their white owners to be used, abused, and sold at the master's whim. At first, white indentured servants and Indian slaves were used for labor in the British colonies. Many, however, fell to diseases such as malaria and yellow fever. Most of the black slaves were immune to these diseases due to a trait now known as Sickle cell anemia. The demand for black slaves, therefore, increased dramatically due to their longevity and agricultural skills acquired in their own lands.

Jazz

Jazz is America's indigenous musical form art that was derived and influenced by the African-American songs of labor and spirituality. Although early records were not kept and there are no recordings of pre-jazz music, it is evident that jazz harmonies, melodies, and rhythms have their roots in African origins. Black traditional music relied heavily on oral transmission and is represented by spirituals, work songs, filed hollers, and later by the blues. When approximately four million slaves became American citizens, their African background blended with the popular music and church songs of the time. It is believed that this became the kernel of American jazz. The word jazz is thought to have come from the early sounds that were associated with brothels and was once thought of as a vulgar term used for sexual acts. It is reported that in 1891, cornettist Buddy Bolden (1877-1931) invented jazz when he picked up his cornet and blew the first notes of jazz. Since his career

was over before the first jazz recordings were made, all that is left of his playing career is legend.

Ragtime is a style of jazz that is characterized by an intricately syncopated rhythm in the melody and an

Famous jazz musician Dizzy Gillespie in 1955.

unfaltering accented accompaniment. From 1900 until 1917, early New Orleans Dixieland used a front line of a cornet, a clarinet and a trombone. A banjo, a tuba, and drums made up the rhythm section. Beginning in the late teens, improvisational music sprang out of the influence that jazz had on dance bands and solo performances. The early jazz of this period has been referred to as Classic Jazz or Traditional Jazz and is associated with the music of Bessie Smith and Clarance Williams. It became the foundation for the musical styles known as Chicago, Kansas City and Swing. It is said that Jazz was born during 1910 and 1920. The Original New Orleans Jazz Band was popular from 1918 to 1919.

The 1920s has been coined the "Jazz Age." The

music of this time period is said to have symbolized the cultural struggle between modernists and traditionalists. It was in part a rejection of what traditionalists thought music was supposed to be while rejecting the Victorian values which dominated nineteenth century American life. New Orleans style Dixieland merged with ragtime to become the Chicago style Dixieland. Chicago became the hub of jazz in the 20s and Louis Armstrong began his influential career as a soloist. Jelly Roll Morton had a hit with his song *Wolverine Blues* in 1923. He and his Red Hot Pepper's band went on to record with the Victor Company until 1930. African-American songwriter Perry Bradford recorded a record of contemporary African-American music with an African-American singer, Mamie Smith and her African-American band, Mamie Smith's Jazz Hounds (1920-1924) . The record was a smash hit and prompted other record companies to jump on the band wagon and start recording African-American Blues and Jazz musicians. It is said that Louis Armstrong first introduced "scat," (the art of creating an improvisation-style instrumental vocally) in 1926 in his song "The Hebbie Jebbies."

Jazz became a popular style following the Great Depression in the 1930s. It reached new levels of sophistication in the Swing Era. Its form has been characterized by its flexible tempos, solo and ensemble improvisations, and sophisticated artistic expressions. It exemplified the need for self-esteem. Count Basie (1904-1984) and Duke Ellington (1899-1974) and their big bands were renown during the Swing Era, as was jazz improviser Django Reinhardt. In the 1940s Bebop was born. It claimed mainstream status although it was not enthusiastically accepted by the jazz community at the time. The military service draft of World War II brought about the break up of the big bands. The music reflected the agitation and the nervousness of the country's mood. Unlike swing, Bebop was not intended for dancing. Artistic styles were stressed over commercial endeavors.

At the end of World War II, beginning in 1947, Bop was replaced with cool jazz and many instruments were used in this music. It was characterized with experimentation in new meters, longer forms, encouraged by the long-playing record, and orchestration. Dizzie Gillespie is a popular Bebop jazz musician. Ella Fitzgerald adopted scat and it became a household word and Sarah Vaughan was able to vocalize many of the notes that Charlie Parker played. In the late 1950s Hard Bop, Funk and Cool jazz take over. Lester Young and Miles Davis are associated with the development of the cool style. Funky Jazz is exemplified by the work of Bobby Timmons with Art Blakely and Cannonball Adderly.

America continued to change, and so did jazz. The looser standards of behavior and the political changes associated with the 1960s was reflected in the avant-garde free jazz form in the music of Cecil Taylor, Ornette Coleman, and Pharoah Sanders. By the 70s, jazz fused with Rock to form Jazz-Rock or Fusion. Miles Davis's "In A Silent Way" and "Bitches Brew" are some of the earliest fusion experiments. Later on Wayne Shorter, Chick Corea, John McLaughlin, and Joe Zawinul became prominent.

In the 1980s, the contemporary jazz age began. Unique individual sounds were heard from Wynton Marsalis, Jeff Watts, Kenny Kirkland, Joshua Redman, John Coltrane, Benny Green and Roy Hargrove, among others. The earthy, bluesy, dance-like rhythms of Jimmy Smith, Shirley Scott, Ramsey Lewis and Stanley Turrentine earned the descriptive label of Soul Jazz. The music of Rhythm and Blues artists King Curtis, Junior Walker, and Earl Bostic is considered jazz-influenced, and Soul Jazz is characterized by the vocals of Nina Simone, and Lou Rawls. The 90s gave way to Hip-Hop and many revivals of jazz's great past.

Today, Jazz is universal. There are many terms to denote its various contemporary forms. Neobop, Afro-Latin Jazz, Acid Jazz, World Fusion Jazz, Neoclassical Jazz and Modern Creative Jazz are terms common in the nineties. And fresh names and faces such as Diane Reeves, Roy Hargrove, and the Freddie Jones Jazz Group are carving out new paths as Jazz continues its history into the year 2000 and beyond.

Beverly Johnson

In 1974, Johnson was the first African-American model to be featured on the cover of *Vogue* magazine. Advertisers soon recognized the growing need for African-American images in advertising to sell merchandise.

James Weldon Johnson

Johnson was the first black to pass the written law examination for Florida bar. His poem "Lift Every Voice and Sing" (1900), set to music by his brother, became the African-American "national anthem" in 1940s. Johnson was foreign consul in Venezuela and Nicaragua from 1906 to 1914. He worked for the NAACP from 1916 to 1930. His books include the fictional *Autobiography of an Ex-Colored Man* (1912), *Book of American Negro Poetry* (1922), *American Negro Spirituals* (1925-26), *Black Manhattan* (1930), autobiographical *Along This Way* (1933), and the philosophical *Negro Americans, What Now* (1934). *God's Trombones* (1927) is a group of dialect sermons in verse.

The Johnson Publishing Company

The Johnson Publishing Company of Chicago, a family-owned conglomerate of media outlets and beauty products, was founded in 1945 by John H. Johnson. In the early 1940s, Johnson collected and prepared a digest of news affecting the African-American community, which was largely ignored by the mainstream press. Johnson used his mother's furniture as collateral to borrow $500, with which he published the first issue of what would be called *Negro Digest*. Similar in form to *Reader's Digest*, *Negro Digest* initially reprinted articles from other periodicals. Soon the magazine began publishing original articles and essays. In October 1943, First Lady Eleanor Roosevelt composed an article especially for *Negro Digest*. That issue doubled the magazine's regular circulation of 50,000. The success of *Negro Digest* led Johnson to launch *Ebony* in 1945. *Ebony* went on to become the keystone of the Johnson Publishing Company and a familiar sight on coffee tables in African-American homes, barber shops, beauty parlors and other gathering spots nationwide. By 1996 its circulation had reached two million. *Negro Digest* remained popular, but its circulation stalled, hovering around 60,000. Johnson discontinued it in 1951. Attempts to revive it in 1965, renaming it *Black World* in 1970, did not suc-

ceed. In its place, Johnson launched *Jet*, a pocket-sized weekly that offered society, entertainment, political, and sports reporting oriented to African-American readers. *Jet* was an immediate success. After six issues, its circulation topped 300,000. By 1997 *Jet's* market covered over 40 countries, and its weekly circulation had climbed to over a million. By the early 1990s, Johnson Publishing employed more than 2,300 people. The total circulation of its publications was 3.25 million, and earnings were $325.7 million in 1996. Johnson's holdings include *Ebony*, *Jet*, *EM: Ebony Man*, and *Ebony South Africa*, Supreme Beauty

John H. Johnson, founder of *Ebony* magazine.

Products, Ebony Fashion Fair, and Johnson Publishing Company Book Division. Today, John H. Johnson continues as publisher and chief executive officer. His wife Eunice W. Johnson is the secretary-treasurer and producer-director of EBONY Fashion Fair. His daughter, Linda Johnson Rice serves as the president and chief operating officer.

Barbara Jordan

After serving in the Texas State Senate, Jordan became the first black congresswoman from the Deep South (1973-79). A spellbinding orator, Jordan gave the keynote address at the 1976 Democratic National Convention.

Michael Jordan

While at the University of North Carolina, Michael Jordan was named All-American and named college basketball player of the year. In 1984 he won Olympic gold with the U.S. national team at the Los Angeles Olympics, the same year he was recruited by the Chicago Bulls basketball team. Jordan was chosen Rookie of the Year in the NBA, and led the Chicago Bulls to record championships. Jordan's performances turned basketball into an international spectator sport. After taking a short leave from basketball following the death of his father, Jordan joined the Chicago Bulls and led the team to two more championships. In addition to his extraordinary success on the court, Jordan had been influential in the sports industry and worked hard for a number of charities.

Jackie Joyner-Kersee

Florence Griffith-Joyner's sister-in-law won the all-around heptathlon at the Seoul Olympic Games in 1988 and the 1992 Barcelona Olympics, winning six Olympic medals overall. She won her sixth Olympic medal in the Atlanta Olympics of 1996, and since her retirement has formed her own sports marketing company and created the Jackie Joyner-Kersee Community Foundation in East St. Louis to help needy children in her hometown. In 1998 she became the first woman named Athlete of the Year by *Sporting News.*

Juba

The juba is a dance that originated in Africa. It was brought to America around the eighteenth century and was customarily performed on plantations in the south during the eighteenth and nineteenth centuries. The juba is a group dance that uses complex rhythmic clapping and animated body movements.

Percy L. Julian

Julian was a Harvard graduate who received a Ph.D. from the University of Vienna. A chemist, who synthesized the drug physostigmine for treatment of glaucoma in 1935, he was also famous for his work developing soya derivatives, firefighting foam used in World War II, and steroids for treatment of arthritis. He formed Julian Laboratories in 1953.

Kansas

By the 1850's, Kansas became the center of national controversy on the issue of slavery. The controversy reached the level of armed warfare among the settlers who included the Abolitionist John Brown. The bloody events led to the name, "bleeding Kansas." Kansas fought in the Civil War with the Union and suffered the highest fatality rate of any northern state.

Kikombe Cha Umoja

The *Kikombe Cha Umoja* is the chalice or cup that holds the Tambiko or beverage that is passed among the family and guests during Kwanzaa. Sharing the Tambiko unites the participants and honors the ancestors.

Kinara

The *Kinara* is the candle holder used during Kwanza. It represents the African-Americans of past generations. It holds seven candles.

Coretta Scott King

During the lifetime of Martin Luther King, Jr., Coretta Scott King worked by her husband's side in the Civil Rights Movement. Born in Alabama,

Coretta Scott King has carried on the civil rights work of her husband, the Rev. Martin Luther King, Jr.

King traveled north to pursue a career in music, but when she married, returned to Alabama to be with King when he became a church pastor. Famous for performing and leading people in song during lectures, she developed the format for freedom concerts. Since King's assassination in 1968, Coretta Scott King has played a major role in civil rights work. She was a major speaker on Solidarity Day in June 1968 and, in the same year, was the first woman commencement speaker at Harvard University. In 1983, King won the Franklin D. Roosevelt Freedom Medal and in 1995 was honored by the National Political Congress of Black Women.

Martin Luther King Jr.

Martin Luther King, Jr. is the best known leader of the Civil Rights Movement which took place in the 1950's and 60's. He was born in Atlanta, Georgia in 1929, the son of Martin Luther, a Baptist minister and Alberta Christine Williams, a teacher. Martin Luther King, Sr. had inherited his ministry at the Ebenezer Baptist Church in Atlanta from his wife's father, Adam Daniel Williams. King learned the ideals of Christian love as well as the African-American Baptist oratory techniques from his father's and grandfather's sermons. He entered Morehouse College in 1944 and then in 1948 began studies at the Crozer Theological Seminary where he was first introduced to the philosophy of passive resistance-non-violent, direct confrontation. King embraced non-violent resistance as the best, most moral and most practical way to achieve social reform in the United States. After finishing his studies at the seminary he began doing Ph.D. work in theology at Boston University. It was during his time in Boston that he married Coretta Scott.

King rose to the head of the Civil Rights Movement rather quickly, brought into the spotlight by his role in the Montgomery Bus Boycott of 1955. It was during his time as president of the Montgomery Improvement Association that King delivered his first civil rights address at Holt Street Baptist Church. The speech urged the boycotters to continue their fight for equal rights, which they did for 382 days. During this time King was arrested, received hate mail and verbal insults, and even had his house bombed. Nevertheless, he managed to maintain his adherence to the philosophy of non-violence, and the protesters won their battle when the Supreme Court declared Montgomery's bus segregation laws to be unconstitutional in 1956.

In 1957 he gathered with other black leaders to form the Southern Christian Leadership Conference (SCLC). The goal of SCLC was to end segregation. To achieve this end, King began an extensive tour of the country, giving speeches and sermons attacking segregation, meeting with various public officials, and writing a book, *Stride Toward Freedom: The Montgomery Story*, which chronicled the experience of the bus boycott in Montgomery and explained King's politics of nonviolence.

King believed that Birmingham, Alabama was the most segregated city in America. Almost every place in the city was segregated, and African-Americans did not have equal opportunities in gaining employment. Local leaders invited King and the SCLC to their city to help them remedy these conditions. They decided to march in protest. King prepared for the march by training the protesters in non-violent techniques. The March ended with King's imprisonment where he wrote "Letter From a Birmingham Jail," a piece that defined the essence of nonviolent protest.

After his release from jail, King rejoined the protestors. This time the demonstrators were children. The viewing public saw police turn on the children with clubs, dogs, tear gas, and high pressure hoses. A national and international cry to end segregation went up. President John F. Kennedy responded to this public outcry, and Birmingham officials agreed to meet King's demands for desegregation and more equal hiring practices. White supremacists were angered and bombed King's hotel and his brother's home.

Martin Luther King, Jr. took the spotlight as head of the Civil Rights Movement during the Montgomery Bus Boycott.

Rioting followed, and federal troops were forced to intervene to stop the violence.

After this victory King became involved in a massive march on Washington that he planned with leaders of other civil rights groups. The goal was to raise national consciousness about the Civil Rights Movement and to urge Congress to pass a civil rights bill that was coming up for a vote. In front of two hundred and fifty thousand people King delivered his famous "I Have a Dream" Speech in front of the Lincoln Memorial. Early in 1964, King stood by as the President signed the Civil Rights Act of 1964, which declared that the federal government was firmly dedicated to ending segregation and discrimination in all public places.

The "I Have a Dream" speech and the signing of the Civil Rights Act marked King's elevation to a position of national and international prominence. This status was confirmed as he became the first black American to be named as *Time* magazine's "Man of the Year" in 1964. In November of the same year he was awarded the Nobel Peace Prize, becoming the youngest person ever to win the award. King spoke against the Vietnam War and on behalf of the poor in urban and rural areas. Then he turned his attentions back to the nation and in 1967 initiated the Poor People's Campaign. His work with the Poor People's Campaign came to a quick end. King was assassinated on April 4, 1968, while staying at a hotel in Memphis to plan a demonstration.

King has been praised as a great man and a martyr. Close friends and family established his birthday as a national holiday. King's memory lives on in his published and collected speeches, essays and books, and the profound changes he effected in American society during his twelve years of working toward civil rights.

The Korean War

The pace of integration in the U. S. armed forces was sluggish. The Marine Corps limited its integration mostly to athletic teams and the Navy funneled 65 percent of its African-American soldiers into the Steward's Branch, where they worked as waiters and cooks. The Army and Air Force continued to train in segregated units. The urgency surrounding the outbreak of the Korean War in June 1950 was instrumental in advancing the integration of the military. At first, the black soldiers who were sent to Korea fought in segregated units. The largest of these was the 24th Infantry Regiment of the 25th Infantry Division, which was ordered into a major battle within a week of arriving in Korea. The 24th Infantry helped push the North Koreans out of Yechon, an important transportation hub, in a victory that later served as a rallying cry for other regiments. A few of the 24th Infantry's soldiers, including Private William Thompson and Sergeant Cornelius Charlton, received the Congressional Medal of Honor for their efforts. Their performance raised questions among army leaders about the effectiveness of segregating battalions by race. The United States' hasty entrance into the war provided a further push toward integration.

Ku Klux Klan

The Ku Klux Klan is an organization that was originally established by former Confederate soldiers in Pulaski, Tennessee in 1866 at the end of the Civil War. The society was committed to maintaining white supremacy in the Southern states where freedom was declared for black slaves. The Klan aimed to suppress the newly acquired rights of the Negroes. It conducted many vigilante acts of violence against black people and the carpetbaggers from the North. The Ku Klux Klan dissolved in 1869 and then resurfaced in 1915. The Klan's anti-black movement has grown to include an anti-Jewish, anti-Catholic, and anti-alien emphasis.

The Ku Klux Klan was formed at the end of the Civil War.

Kwanzaa

This African-American holiday has been observed since its inception in 1966 by Black Studies professor, Dr. Maulana Karenga. It is celebrated between December 26th and January 1st. The word *Kwanzaa* means "the first" or "the first fruits of the harvest," in the East African language of Kiswahili. There are seven special symbols associated with Kwanzaa. They adorn the Kwanzaa table.

At the heart of the meaning and activities of Kwanzaa are the *Nguzo Saba* (the Seven Principles): *umoja* (unity), *kujichagulia* (self-determination), *ujima* (collective work and responsibility), *ujamaa* (cooperative economics), *nia* (purpose), *kuumba* (creativity), and *imani* (faith). Each day of Kwanzaa is dedicated to one of the principles and is organized around activities and discussion to emphasize that principle.

Kwanzaa Symbols

At each evening meal during Kwanzaa, family members light one of the *mishumaa saba* (seven candles), to focus on the principles. The *mazao* (crops), are symbolic of African harvest celebrations and of the rewards of collective labor. The *mkeka* (mat) symbolizes tradition and history. The *kinara* (candleholder) is symbolic of ancestral roots, or continental Africans. *Muhindi* (corn) symbolizes children. The *kikombe cha umoja* (unity cup), is symbolic of the foundational principle and practice of unity; and *zawadi* (gifts) symbolize the labor and love of parents. There are also two supplemental symbols: a representation of the *Nguzo Saba* and the *bendera* (flag), which contains the colors black, red, and green. These colors are symbolic, respectively, of African people, their struggle, and the promise and future that come from their struggle.

Leadbelly

Born Huddie William Ledbetter near Shreveport, La., probably on Jan. 21, 1885, Leadbelly became a wandering musician who sang the blues. He was imprisoned for six years on murder charges, before being pardoned in 1918. John and Alan Lomax, who were collecting folk songs for the Library of Congress, discovered him on a Louisiana prison farm in 1930. "On Top of Old Smoky" and "Good Night, Irene," became hits after his death in 1949.

Spike Lee

Born Shelton Jackson Lee in Atlanta, Ga., in 1957, director-writer-actor Lee won a student Academy Award for *Joe's Bed-Stuy Barbershop: We Cut Heads* (his thesis at New York University's film school). His first commercial film was the low-budget black-and-white *She's Gotta Have It* (1986). His other films include *Do the Right Thing* (1989), *Mo' Better Blues* (1990), *Jungle Fever* (1991), *Malcolm X* (1992), *Clockers* (1995) and *Get on the Bus* (1996). Lee's work features scores by his father, jazz musician-composer Bill Lee. A completely original talent, Lee spotlighted contemporary African-American life. His production company is named Forty Acres and a Mule for the free African-American's unfulfilled Reconstruction dream.

Carl Lewis

In 1984, Carl Lewis became the first athlete, since Jesse Owens in 1936, to win four gold medals in Olympic competition. He broke several Olympic records and won gold in every Olympic up until his retirement from competition in 1997. He was inducted into the Olympic Hall of Fame in 1985.

Literature

As early as Colonial times in America, African-Americans contributed to literature. The slave narratives were among the most important. Protest writings were another form of literature produced by slaves. White literature usually portrayed black people in stereotypes. Early in the twentieth century, most publishers and readers in the United States were still white, and a controversy developed over the degree to which the perceived expectations of the white establishment should be met. Many African-American writers felt that whites, interested only in stereotypical portrayals of blacks as primitive, were unduly fascinated by the more sensational aspects of Harlem and African-American sexuality. While this primitivism was rejected by some African-American authors as a destructive stereotype, it was actually fostered by others who considered it a continuation of African custom and a defiance of white Puritanism. Among the poets who embraced primitivism was Arna Bontemps.

At the same time, growing interest among white Americans in jazz and blues music and the discovery of some African sculpture by modernist artists broadened the audience for African-American writing. Some black critics, including DuBois and Benjamin Brawley, welcomed the increase in white patronage and stressed the value of literature in fostering racial equality. Others, including Alain Locke and Charles W. Chesnutt, decried such overt use of literature for propaganda purposes. While few black critics asserted the complete independence of art from social concerns, most believed that literature could best promote racial equality by showing that black writers could produce works rivaling or surpassing those of their white counterparts.

Continuing work he had begun at the beginning of the century, DuBois produced books and essays on the position of African-Americans in this country and on the steps African-Americans needed to take to achieve equality. The appearance of African-American journals such as DuBois's *Crisis* and Charles S. Johnson's *Opportunity* made it much easier for black writers to publish in a style that suited their tastes.

Johnson, with his influential anthology of verse, *Book of American Negro Poetry* (1922) set the manipulation of language and other patterns of signification as the heart of the African-American poetic enterprise. Thus, literature of the era was marked by a shift away from moralizing and political ideals, which had been characteristic of much post- Reconstruction writing.

Lynching

In the United States lynching has been used against members of many different ethnicities. However, the vast majority of victims have been African-American men, mostly in the Southern states, during a 50-year period following Reconstruction. Lynching became a tragic symbol of race relations in the American South, used to maintain the status quo of white superiority long after any legal distinction between the races remained. Lynching cast a shadow greater than its 3,386 known black (mostly male) victims between 1882 and 1930. It is almost certain that these numbers are understated. Many cases were never recorded, and even those that were well documented rarely reveal the names of the perpetrators.

Lynching had its roots in the lawless early days of pre-Revolutionary America, a means of controlling people deemed marginal by society's mainstream. Although slaves were brutalized and sometimes killed by white slaveholders, systematic violence against African-Americans in the form of lynching was not prevalent before the Civil War.

Although accurate statistics on lynching were not kept before 1882, historians believe that the numbers grew throughout the 1870s and 1880s, peaking around 1892. From that year on, white victims of mob execution sharply and steadily decreased, while blacks in the South continued to be lynched in large numbers (for instance, in 1900, 106 African-Americans were lynched, compared to 9 whites). From its frontier roots, when it took the place of legal law enforcement, lynching became almost entirely a Southern, racial

Lynching, which reached its height in the period between 1882 and 1930, did not die out until the 1960s.

phenomenon. Ida B. Wells-Barnett, an African-American woman published several influential pamphlets detailing the horrors of lynching in the early 1890s. In 1909, when the National Association for the Advancement of Colored People (NAACP) was founded, an end to lynching was named as one of the organization's top priorities from the start. In 1917 the NAACP staged the Negro Silent Protest Parade in New York City to criticize the federal government's lack of commitment to ending lynching. The Dyer Bill, which would have made participating in a lynch mob a federal crime, was first introduced in 1918 by Leonidas Dyer, a white Republican congressman from Missouri. Over the next ten years, the NAACP, led by James Weldon Johnson and Walter White, lobbied heavily for its passage, which was repeatedly blocked by Southern Democrats in the Senate. Despite its legislative failure, the Dyer Bill debate allowed the NAACP to educate the white American public about the amount and severity of racial violence that was going unpunished. The number of lynchings began to decrease in the twentieth century, especially during the 1920s; by the late 1930s, the annual victim count was in the single digits. Although some African-Americans were still lynched in the following decades, lynching more or less ended by 1965.

Magazines

Freedom's Journal was the first African-American newspaper in the United States. Its editors, Samuel Cornish and John Brown Russwurm, proposed in their first editorial that their paper, a weekly, would provide an opportunity for black people to speak for themselves rather than be represented by whites. *Freedom's Journal* was a strong proponent of the abolition of slavery, and Cornish and Russwurm often employed black abolitionists. *The Liberator* was an antislavery newspaper published from 1831 to 1865 and edited by William Lloyd Garrison, a prominent white abolitionist.

The *Journal of Negro History* was a quarterly publication founded by African-American historian and educator Carter G. Woodson to correct white racist views of African-American history and culture. Woodson published the first issue of *Journal of Negro History* in January 1916. Another magazine of the

time, *The Guardian*, or *Boston Guardian*, edited by William Monroe Trotter, challenged Booker T. Washington's philosophy of accommodation.

During the Harlem Renaissance, several agencies had magazines that published work by young black writers and sponsored writing contests. Two such periodicals were *The Crisis*, published by the national Association for the Advancement of Colored People (NAACP) and edited by DuBois, and *Opportunity*, published by the Urban League and edited by Charles S. Johnson. Independent magazines, such as *The Messenger*–a militant socialist journal edited by A. Philip Randolph and Chandler Owen–published up and coming African-American writers. Some writers, such as Wallace Thurman, Langston Hughes, Zora Neale Hurston, Aaron Douglas, John P. Davis, Bruce Nugent, and Gwendolyn Bennett, even tried to start their own literary journal, *Fire!!*, which lasted only one issue.

Since the 1940s, the Johnson Company has responsible for the most popular magazines addressed to African-Americans. *Negro Digest*, *Ebony*, *Jet*, and *Ebony Man* among others. *Essence* is the African-American women's magazine, founded in 1970, focusing on health, beauty, fashion, fiction, self-improvement, and issues of interest to contemporary upscale black women. *Black Enterprise* was also founded in 1970 by publisher and editor Earl Graves, Sr. The magazine has a strong emphasis on economic cooperation among African-Americans, community activitism, and solutions to black financial problems that are outside of the traditional strategies of corporate America. It features stories about successful African-American businesses.

Malcolm X
(né Malcolm Little; Islamic name: El-Hajj Malik El-Shabazz)

Malcolm Little followed the teachings of the Honorable Elijah Muhammad and underwent a spiritual awakening and conversion to the Black Muslim faith while in prison. He also rejected the surname given to his family by his ancestor's slave owner and adopted the surname "X," signifying his lost and unknown African family name. Malcolm's oratory skills were soon recognized, and in 1954, Elijah Muhammad moved him to Harlem's prominent Temple (Mosque) Seven, where he gained prominence as the primary spokesperson for the Black Muslims across the nation.

Malcolm believed that the goals of racial equality and integration were unworthy goals in a racist nation. He called for African-Americans to work together, independently from European Americans, to form their own businesses, schools, and communities. He advocated patronizing businesses run by African-Americans and avoiding or boycotting businesses run by racists of other races. Malcolm called for African-Americans to take pride in their own distinctive cultural heritage. He opposed the nonviolent struggle for civil rights as an ineffectual means of gaining equality and integration. Though he never advocated violence as a form of aggression, he did say that African-Americans should defend themselves and their communities "by any means necessary," including violent means.

Malcolm X addressing a Harlem rally in 1963.

Malcolm X directed the establishment of two universities of Islam, providing a Black Muslim education to school age children in Detroit and Chicago. He also founded many new mosques, recruited new members, and lectured around the nation. In 1961, he founded the official publication of the Nation of Islam, *Muhammad Speaks*. He was soon considered second only to Elijah Muhammad in the Nation of Islam.

Malcolm was an extremely devoted follower until he become aware of Muhammad's envy, sexual promiscuity, and excessive use of Muslim resources for his own material gain. Following the assassination of President John Kennedy, Malcolm remarked that this was a "case of chickens coming home to roost," meaning that the violence of powerful white men was being turned back against them. He was chastised by Muhammad for his cavalier attitude and ordered to be silent for 90 days. Malcolm complied obediently, but his period of silence allowed him to reflect on his allegiance to a leader who so betrayed what he believed to be the core principles of Islam.

Malcolm split from the Nation of Islam and organized his own Muslim Mosque, Inc., in Harlem. He also decided to dedicate himself to traditional Islam, as it is practiced throughout the world. In April 1964, Malcolm made his first haj. This was his second spiritual awakening which he shared with fellow Moslems from Asia, Africa, Europe, and the Americas. He realized that whites were not by nature evil, but that racism was the evil he righteously hated. Instead of advocating racial division and separatism, he wished to promote international solidarity to overcome the evils of racism. He changed his name from Malcolm X to the Arabic name El-Hajj Malik El-Shabazz.

On his return to the United States, El-Shabazz formed the secular Organization of Afro-American Unity (OAAU), to promote African-American cultural pride through an internationalist framework of brotherhood, linking Africans, Asians, and Americans of all racial and cultural heritages. He was soon traveling throughout the Middle East, Africa, and Europe, giving speeches reflecting his new worldly attitude, urging others around the world to help African-Americans in the fight against racism and oppression. He also spoke to the United Nations in New York, charging the United States with denying human rights to African-Americans.

Once he embraced orthodox Islam and renounced the Nation of Islam as inauthentic, the hostility between him and the Nation intensified. Threats of violence assaulted him and his family at an increasing rate. On February 21, 1965, when he was addressing an OAAU rally at the Audubon Ballroom in Harlem, he was assassinated. Three Black Muslims were later convicted of his murder.

Months before Malcolm X broke with Elijah Muhammad, he had begun working with Alex Haley to write his autobiography. In the autobiography, Malcolm was surprisingly frank, candidly revealing his own past crimes and misdeeds. Since his death, many

A dramatic moment at the March on Washington in 1963.

of his key speeches have also been published, such as in the collections *Malcolm X Speaks: Selected Speeches and Statements* (1965) and *By Any Means Necessary: Speeches, Interviews, and a Letter* (1970), and *The Speeches of Malcolm X at Harvard* (1968).

March on Washington 1963

The 1963 March on Washington attracted an estimated 250,000 people for a massive, peaceful demonstration to promote Civil Rights and economic equality for African-Americans. Participants walked down Constitution and Independence avenues. Then gathered before the Lincoln Monument for speeches, songs, and prayer. Televised live to an audience of millions, the march provided dramatic moments, most memorably the Rev Martin Luther King Jr.'s "I Have a Dream" speech. Far larger than previous demonstrations for any cause, the march had an obvious impact, both on the passage of civil rights legislation and on nationwide public opinion. It proved the power of mass appeal and inspired imitators in the antiwar, feminist, and environmental movements. It was the high point of the Civil Rights Movement. The march was initiated by A. Philip Randolph, international presi-

dent of the Brotherhood of Sleeping Car Porters, president of the Negro American Labor Council, and vice president of the AFL-CIO; and sponsored by five of the largest civil rights organizations in the United States. Known in the press as "the big six," the major players were Randolph; Whitney Young, president of the National Urban League (NUL); Roy Wilkins, president of the National Association for the Advancement of Colored People (NAACP); James Farmer, founder and president of the Congress of Racial Equality (CORE); John Lewis, president of the Student Nonviolent Coordinating Committee (SNCC); and Martin Luther King Jr. founder and president of the Southern Christian Leadership Conference (SCLC). Bayard Rustin, a close associate of Randolph's and organizer of the first Freedom Ride in 1947, orchestrated and administered the details of the march. On August 28th the marchers arrived. They came in chartered buses and private cars, on trains and planes. One man even roller-skated to Washington from Chicago. By 11 o'clock in the morning, more than 200,000 had gathered by the Washington Monument, where the march was to begin. It was a diverse crowd: black and white, rich and poor, young and old, Hollywood stars and ordinary people. Despite the fears that had prompted extraordinary precautions (including pre-signed executive orders authorizing

Scene from the March on Washington.

military intervention in the case of rioting), those assembled marched peacefully to the Lincoln Monument. After the national anthem and an invocation by Archbishop Patrick O'Boyle came the speeches. John Lewis, the 23-year-old president of SNCC, promised that without "meaningful legislation" blacks would "march through the South." When Mahalia Jackson took the stage to sing "I've Been 'Buked and I've Been Scorned," the crowd was moved. King, the last speaker of the day, was introduced by Randolph as "the moral leader of our nation." With the passionate, poetic style he had honed as a preacher, King electrified the audience and built to his "I have a dream" finale. The rally concluded with Rustin's reading of the march's ten demands. These included not only passage of the civil rights bill but also school and housing desegregation, job training, and an increase in the minimum wage. The marchers' pledge was also read, followed by a benediction from Dr. Benjamin E. Mays, president of Morehouse College. The march ended at 4:20 in the afternoon. As marchers returned to the buses that would take them home, the organizers met with President Kennedy, who encouraged them to continue with their work.

Wynton Marsalis

Marsalis emerged as one of the great trumpeters of the late twentieth century, winning Grammy awards for both his jazz and classical works. His brother, Branford, became music director for television's popular *Tonight Show* in 1992.

Thurgood Marshall

As staff lawyer for the NAACP and as its chief counsel for the Legal Defense and Education Fund, Marshall presented winning arguments before the Supreme Court in many civil rights cases, including historic Brown v Board of Education of Topeka (1954). He was appointed United States solicitor general in 1965. Marshall served on the Supreme Court from 1967 to 1991. He was the first African-American appointed to the court.

The Middle Passage

The Middle Passage is the term used to describe the transatlantic slave voyages between Africa and the Americas that claimed the lives of approximately 1.8 million slaves over a period of about 350 years. An estimated 12 million slaves were packed like animals aboard slave vessels. This middle, or second leg of the transatlantic slave trade marked the beginning of a terrifying experience. Typically, slaves were shackled in pairs, the right arm and leg of one chained to the left arm and leg of the other. Men were separated from women, but all were confined below deck and packed into slave quarters throughout the ship's belly. These quarters were no more 6 feet long and not high enough to allow an individual to sit upright. Slaves were forced to lie naked on wooden planks, and many developed bruises and open sores. The unsanitary conditions were breeding grounds for diseases, such as smallpox, dysentery, and measles. Close to 5 percent of the slaves aboard these vessels died from disease, and many more died from malnutrition. Slaves were fed twice a day rations of fish, beans, or yams that were prepared in large copper vats below deck. Those who refused to eat, hoping to starve themselves to death, were force-fed. Slaves were sometimes allowed, in small groups, to come on deck for exercise. Women and children were often permitted to roam freely, a practice that opened opportunities for the ship's crew to abuse and rape them. Occasionally some slaves managed to break free from their shackles and organize mutinies. Over 250 cases of rebellion at sea are documented. Some captives jumped overboard to escape slavery.

Doris (Dorie) Miller

African-American Dorie Miller had the distinction of being the first American hero of World War II. Dorie was working as a messman on the USS *Arizona* when it was docked in Pearl Harbor on December 7, 1941. He had no prior experience with antiaircraft guns, because at that time, the navy did not include blacks in gunnery training. But when the unexpected attack on the *Arizona* occurred that day, Miller independently took control of a gun and brought down four Japanese planes. Although the *Arizona* did eventually sink, Miller was recognized for his bravery and heroic action and he was given the Navy Cross.

In spite of his courageous efforts, however, Miller was never acknowledged as a navy gunner. He died as a messman during an attack on the aircraft carrier, *Liscome Bay*.

Million-Man March

The Million Man March was a rally organized by Nation of Islam minister Louis Farrakhan and former NAACP director Benjamin Chavis on October 16, 1995, in Washington, D.C. The Million Man March emerged from a call from Farrakhan for a Day of Atonement that would draw attention to the social and economic problems plaguing African-American males. Approximately 900,000 black men gathered in Washington, D.C., to hear speeches from black leaders such as Rosa Parks, Jesse Jackson, and Maya Angelou. Farrakhan provided the keynote address. He asked black men to assume responsibility for themselves, their families, their communities, and America as a whole. He told them not to place the blame for their conditions on outside forces. The Million Man March was the largest gathering of African-Americans in history, surpassing in size the 1963 March on Washington. It eventually led to a Million Woman March in Philadelphia, Pennsylvania on October 25, 1997.

Mishumaasba

The *Mishumaasba* are the seven candles that are placed in the Kwanzaa candle holder. There are three red candles placed on the right, three green candles placed on the left, and one black candle in the middle. On the first day of Kwanzaa, the black candle is lit. On the second day, a green candle is lit. On the third day, a red candle is lit. A green candle is lit on the fourth day; a red candle is lit on the fifth day. On the sixth day, a green candle is lit and on the last day a red candle is lit.

Montgomery Bus Boycott

The Montgomery Bus Boycott of 1955 was initially organized by a number of black activist groups who came together to protest the arrest of Rosa Parks,

An empty bus during the Montgomery boycott.

an African-American woman who had been arrested for refusing to give up her seat on a city bus to a white passenger (as the segregation laws required her to do). These groups all joined together to create the Montgomery Improvement Association, a group which was supposed to work with city and bus line officers to establish better treatment of blacks in Montgomery. They elected Martin Luther King, Jr. as the MIA's first president.

Toni Morrison

In 1993, Toni Morrison became the first black woman to receive the Nobel Prize for Literature. Her works are noted for their powerful storytelling, provocative themes, and poetic language. Morrison's novels explore racial and gender conflicts and the various ways that people express their identities. Her novels include *The Bluest Eye* (1970), *Song of Solomon* (1977), *Jazz* (1992), and *Sula* (1973). *Sula* was nominated for the 1975 National Book Award in fiction.

Song of Solomon brought Morrison national attention, winning the National Book Critic's Circle Award and the American Academy and Institute of Arts and Letters Award. In 1980, President Jimmy Carter appointed Morrison to the National Council on the Arts. The next year she published her fourth novel, *Tar Baby*. For the first time, she described the interaction between black and white characters, exploring conflicts of race, class, and gender.

Morrison continued to forge her place in American literary history. Her picture appeared on the cover of the March 30, 1981 issue of *Newsweek* magazine. Her first play, *Dreaming Emmett*, was based on the true story of Emmett Till, a black teenager killed by racist whites in 1955 after being accused of making a snide remark to a white woman. The play premiered January 4, 1986 at the Marketplace Theater in Albany.

Morrison's next novel, *Beloved*, was published in 1987 and became a bestseller. In 1988 it won the Pulitzer prize for fiction, and in 1998 was made into a movie. In 1987, Morrison was named the Robert F. Goheen Professor in the Council of Humanities at Princeton University. She became the first black woman writer to hold a named chair at an Ivy League University. She taught creative writing and also took part in the African-American studies, American Studies and women's studies programs.

Motown Records

Founded in 1959 in Detroit, Michigan by Berry Gordy, Jr., Motown Records became the biggest black-owned business in the United States, delivering black music and black performers to the mainstream of popular music. The Motown sound was an influential force in popular black music through the 1960s. It was a blend of gospel and pop and appealed to both black and white audiences. The music was distinguished by its distinctive genre, its catchy refrains, and highly stylized arrangements.

In 1964 and 1965, Motown Records had five number one hits by the Supremes on the *Billboard* charts. By 1967, Motown Records was creating music history with the Supremes, Stevie Wonder, Smokey Robinson, the Four Tops, Gladys Knight and the Pips, Martha and the Vandellas, the Temptations, Mary Wells, and Marvin Gaye. In 1971, Motown Records was relocated to Los Angeles where Berry Gordy had hits with Stevie Wonder, the Jackson Five, Lionel Richie, the Commodores and Rick James.

By this time, Motown was no longer the trend setting company it had been in the decade before. MCA record company bought Motown Records in 1988 and under the direction of Jheryl Busby it emerged with the sounds of Boyz II Men. Their song "End of the Road" was number one on the *Billboard* charts for an unprecedented 13 weeks in 1992. The Motown Record Company was bought by the Polygram Group in 1993.

Elijah Muhammad

Elijah Muhammad was born Elijah Poole in 1897. In 1931, Elijah attended his first Islamic meeting and met its leader Wallace D. Fard. He became fully immersed in the movement, abandoning his "slave-owner" surname. Within the year he became Fard's top assistant. In 1933, Fard named Muhammad

Supreme Minister, and the following year Muhammad succeeded him as head of the black separatist Nation of Islam. Muhammad purchased radios, modern farm equipment, and 140 acres of farmland, a grocery store, restaurant, and a bakery. He purchased cars and real estate and apparently had sexual liaisons with a number of young women in the movement. He served a jail sentence for draft evasion during World War II and was wired by the FBI for over two decades. When Malcolm X was murdered after leaving the movement, there were many who believed that Muhammad's violent denunciation of his one-time protege instigated the assassination. Nevertheless, by the time of his death in 1975, his conservative approach made him seem moderate compared to other radical groups of the Civil Rights era.

Muhindi

The *Muhindi* are the ears of corn used during the Kwanzaa holiday. The ears of corn pose as the children in the home. The corn embodies the life cycle and honors fertility. It celebrates the generations of African-American families in the past, in the present, and in the future.

Eddie Murphy

Edward Regan Murphy, born in Brooklyn, New York in 1969, received his first film break in 1982 when he appeared in *49 Hours*, a film that became an instant hit. He followed with roles in *Trading Places* (1983), and had the starring role in *Beverly Hills Cop* (1985). Murphy became a superstar, and although his career dipped in the early 1990s, he made a comeback in 1996 with the release of *The Nutty Professor*, which grossed over $100 million. He received a Golden Globe Award and the NAACP Image Award, and Emmy nominations for his appearance in *Saturday Night Live*. In 1991 he received the NAACP's Lifetime Achievement Award, and an *Essence Magazine* Spirit Award in 1994. Murphy has his own star on the Hollywood Walk of Fame.

Walter Dean Myers

Walter Dean Myers is a prolific award-winning author of fiction and non-fiction books for children and young adults. The Children's Book Council first recognized him on Interracial Books for Children in 1969 for his book, *Where Does the Day Go*. Since then he has won numerous acknowledgments from the American Library Association, and has been given the Coretta Scott King Award for *Now Is Your Time, Scorpions, Motown and Didi, A Love Story, The Young Landlords*, and *Malcolm X*. He received the Newberry Honor Award for *Somewhere in the Darkness*, and *Scorpions*. His son Christopher illustrated *Harlem*, a book of Walter's poetry. It is a Caldecott Honor Book.

National Association for the Advancement of Colored People (NAACP)

An interracial membership organization founded in 1909, the NAACP has been devoted to civil rights and racial justice. Throughout its existence the NAACP forged a middle road of interracial cooperation and has worked primarily through the American legal system to fulfill its goals. The NAACP was formed in response to the 1908 race riot in Springfield, Illinois, birthplace of President Abraham Lincoln. Appalled at the violence that was committed against blacks, a group of white liberals that included Mary White Ovington and Oswald Garrison Villard, both the descendants of abolitionists, issued a call for a meeting. Some 60 people, only seven of whom were

African-American (including W. E. B. Du Bois, Ida B. Wells-Barnett, and Mary Church Terrell), signed the call. The NAACP's goal was to secure for all people the rights guaranteed in the 13th, 14th, and 15th Amendments to the United States Constitution, which promised an end to slavery, the equal protection of the law, and universal adult male suffrage, respectively.

The NAACP established its national office in New York City and named as president, Moorfield Storey, a white constitutional lawyer and former president of the American Bar Association. DuBois, the only African-American among the organization's executives, was made director of publications and research. In 1910 he established the official journal of the NAACP, *The Crisis*. A series of early court battles helped establish the NAACP's importance as a legal advocate. The organization won its first court battle in1915 against D. W. Griffith's inflammatory *Birth of a Nation*, a motion picture that perpetuated demeaning stereotypes of African-Americans and glorified the Ku Klux Klan.

The NAACP's membership grew rapidly, from around 9,000 in 1917 to around 90,000 in 1919, with more than 300 local branches. The writer and diplomat James Weldon Johnson became the association's first black secretary in 1920, and Louis T. Wright, a surgeon, was named the first African-American chairman of its board of directors in 1934. In 1930 the association commissioned the Margold Report, which became the basis for its successful reversal of the separate-but-equal doctrine that had governed public facilities since 1896's Plessy v. Ferguson. In 1935 board secretary Walter F. White recruited Charles H. Houston as NAACP chief counsel. Houston was the Howard University law school dean whose strategy on school-segregation cases paved the way for his protégé Thurgood Marshall to prevail in 1954's Brown v. Board of Education, the decision that overturned Plessy.

During the Great Depression of the 1930s, the NAACP began to focus on economic justice. The association cooperated with the newly formed Congress of Industrial Organizations (CIO) in an effort to win jobs for black Americans. President Franklin D. Roosevelt agreed to open thousands of jobs to African-American workers when the NAACP supported labor leader A. Philip Randolph and his March on Washington movement in 1941. Throughout the

1940s the NAACP continued to act as a legislative and legal advocate, pushing for an end to state-mandated segregation. By the 1950s the NAACP's Legal Defense and Educational Fund, headed by Marshall, secured this goal through Brown v. Board of Education (1954), which outlawed segregation in public schools. The NAACP's Washington, D.C., bureau, led by lobbyist Clarence M. Mitchell Jr., helped advance not only integration of the armed forces in 1948 but also passage of the Civil Rights Acts of 1957, 1964, and 1968, as well as the Voting Rights Act of 1965. The Civil Rights Movement of the 1950s and 1960s echoed the NAACP's moderate, integrationist goals. Though the NAACP was opposed to extralegal popular actions, many of its members, such as Mississippi field secretary Medgar Evers, participated in nonviolent demonstrations such as sit-ins to protest the persistence of Jim Crow segregation throughout the South. Although it was criticized for working exclusively within the system, the NAACP did provide legal representation and aid to members of more militant protest groups. Led by Roy Wilkins, who served as secretary in 1955, the NAACP cooperated with organizers A. Philip Randolph and Bayard Rustin in planning the 1963 March on Washington. With the passage of civil rights legislation the following year, the association had finally accomplished much of its historic legislative agenda. Wilkins retired as executive director in 1977 and was replaced by Benjamin L. Hooks, whose tenure included the Bakke case (1978), in which a California court outlawed several aspects of affirmative action. At the end of the twentieth century, the NAACP focused on economic development and educational programs for youths, while also continuing its role as legal advocate for civil rights issues. Kweisi Mfume, former congressman and head of the Congressional Black Caucus, is president and chief executive officer, and Julian Bond is chairman of the board. The organization currently has more than 500,000 members.

National Association of Colored Women

National Association of Colored Women was the first national African-American organization in the United States. The NACW grew out of a network of local African-American women's organizations that developed in the late nineteenth century to promote racial progress by providing social services in black communities. In 1957, the NACW changed its name to the National Association of Colored Women's Clubs. The NACWC celebrated its centennial in 1996, with approximately 40,000 members in 1,500 clubs.

The National Council of Negro Women

One of the largest and most prominent African-American women's groups of the twentieth century, the National Council of Negro Women (NCNW) was founded by civil rights leader Mary McLeod Bethune in 1935. NCNW delegates were present at the founding of the United Nations, and have since attended all United Nations proceedings as official observers. By the mid-1950s, the Council's 11 national departments included Archives and Museum, Citizenship Education, Education, Fine Arts, Human Relations, International Relations, Labor and Industry, Public Relations, Religious Education, Social Welfare, and Youth Conservation.

National Negro Business League

Booker T. Washington founded the National Negro Business League in 1900. It was based in Tuskegee, Alabama from 1899 to 1923. Composed of men and women from around the country, the purpose of the League was to improve the economic situation of African-Americans. Washington wanted to build up the black community internally so that it would be more highly regarded by white Americans. Booker T. Washington sought to implement a strategy for self-help and racial solidarity through racial advancement. The NNBL became an important part of the Tuskegee Machine. It wanted to demonstrate a model of success that African-American business people would emulate.

National Urban League

This not-for-profit community-based civil rights and social services organization was established in 1910. Its mission is to assist African-Americans who are striving to enter the economic mainstream and to help them to achieve social and economic equality and self-sufficiency.

Hugh B. Price became the seventh President and Chief Executive Officer of the National Urban league on July 1, 1994. Under Price's leadership, the National Urban League has worked to encourage the African-American community to solve its own problems by relying on its own strengths and resources. Price has also helped to restore the League's fiscal health by enlarging its endowment and restructuring and strengthening its board of directors and staff. Price has been instrumental in defining the Urban League's vision, role and priorities. He conceived and launched the League's historic Campaign for African-American Achievement in partnership with the Congress of National Black Churches and nearly two dozen national black civic, social, and professional organizations. Price initiated "Achievement Matters," a public service campaign in conjunction with State Farm Life Insurance Company and the National Newspaper Publishers Association. He worked to revive Opportunity, the League's landmark publication, and he supported the establishment of the National Urban League's new headquarters on Wall Street in New York City. The League has 113 affiliates in thirty-four states and Washington, D. C., and serves over two million people a year.

Negro League Baseball

American baseball at its beginnings was a white-only game. During the height of the Jim Crow period—from 1890 to 1920—successful African-American baseball teams played outside of formal leagues, facing any team in the nation that would play them. Various other Negro leagues flourished until the 1940s. Professional teams started forming in the 1880s, including the Philadelphia Orions (1882), the St. Louis Black Stockings (1882), and the Cuban Giants (1885). Under the management of S. K. Govern, the Cuban Giants were immensely successful.

In February 1920, star pitcher Rube Foster founded the Negro National League (NNL) with the owners/representatives of Indianapolis ABCs, the Chicago Giants, the Kansas City Monarchs, the St. Louis Giants, the Detroit Stars, and the Cuban Stars. With players such as sluggers Oscar Charleston, John Henry Lloyd, and the great Smokey Joe Williams, the new, mostly midwestern league garnered fanfare and popular support in African-American communities. In 1923, the Eastern Colored League (ECL) was formed by white booking agent Nat Strong. The two best teams met for a black World Series. In 1932 black baseball thrived mainly in the Southern Negro League, and in Latin America, where great ballplayers were welcome, regardless of race. In the 1930s, the Negro League boasted some of the best baseball talent to ever play the game. The Pittsburgh possessed five future Hall of Fame players at one time: Oscar Charleston, Cool Papa Bell, Josh Gibson, Judy Johnson, and Satchel Paige.

In the spring of 1947 Jackie Robinson entered the Brooklyn Dodgers lineup, becoming the first African-American to play major league baseball since Moses Fleetwood "Fleet" Walker and his brother Weldy played for Toledo, Ohio, in 1884. The National Negro Leagues folded in 1948, due in great part to Robinson's integration of the major leagues. Former Negro leaguers were now playing major league baseball. These players included Paige Monte Irvin, Roy Campanella, Hank Aaron, and Willie Mays.

The Kansas City Monarchs, stars of the Negro League.

Network Newscasters

Ed Bradley has been one of the *60 Minutes* interviewers since 1981. Bryant Gumbel became co-host of *The Today Show* in 1982. Charlayne Hunter-Gault has appeared regularly on the *MacNeil-Lehrer News Hour*. Jennifer Lawson is a vice-president of the Public Broadcasting Service. By the 1990s the talk about late-night talk shows centered on the innovative Arsenio Hall.

The New Deal

Virtually ignored by the Republican administrations of the 1920s, black voters drifted to the Democratic Party, especially in the Northern cities. In the presidential election of 1928 blacks voted in large numbers for the Democrats for the first time. In 1930 Republican President Herbert Hoover nominated John J. Parker, a man of pronounced anti-black views, to the United States Supreme Court. The NAACP successfully opposed the nomination. In the 1932 presidential race blacks overwhelmingly supported the successful Democratic candidate, Franklin D. Roosevelt. The Roosevelt Administration's accessibility to black leaders and the New Deal reforms strengthened black support for the Democratic Party. Many black leaders, members of a so-called "black Cabinet," were advisers to Roosevelt. Among them were the educator Mary McLeod Bethune, who served as the National Youth Administration's director of Negro affairs; William H. Hastie, who in 1937 became the first black federal judge; Eugene K. Jones, executive secretary of the National Urban League; Robert Vann, editor of the Pittsburgh Courier; and the economist Robert C. Weaver.

Although discrimination by local administrators was common, blacks benefited greatly from New Deal programs. Low-cost public housing was made available to black families. The National Youth Administration and the Civilian Conservation Corps enabled black youths to continue their education. The Work Projects Administration gave jobs to many blacks, and its Federal Writers Project supported the work of many authors, among them Zora Neale Hurston, Arna Bontemps, Waters Turpin, and Melvin B. Tolson.

The Congress of Industrial Organizations (CIO), established in the mid-1930s, organized large numbers of black workers into labor unions for the first time. By 1940, there were more than 200,000 blacks in the CIO, many of them officers of union locals.

Nguzu Saba

The Nguzu Saba is the seven basic principles of Kwanzaa. One principle is designated for each of the seven days of the holiday. The seven principles are Umoja - Unity, Kujichagulia - Self Determination, Ujuma - Collective Work and Responsibility, Ujamaa - Cooperative Economics, Nia - Purpose, Kuumba - Creativity, and Imani - Faith.

Niagara Movement

The Niagara Movement was an organization established in Niagara Falls, Canada in 1905 by African-Americans who met secretly to contend with

The original leaders of the Niagra Movement.

racial discrimination. The movement was led by University Professor, W.E.B. DuBois, and it included 29 other prominent blacks who called for full civil liberties, political rights, the abolition of racial discrimination, and social rights for black Americans. The movement held whites accountable for the racial problems in the United States. While the Niagara Movement had 30 branches in a variety of U.S. cities, and it had a few local civil rights victories, the principals of the organization were never fully embraced by many blacks. In 1909, many of the ideas of the Niagara Movement were adopted by the National Association for the Advancement of Colored People. The Niagara Movement was disbanded in 1910.

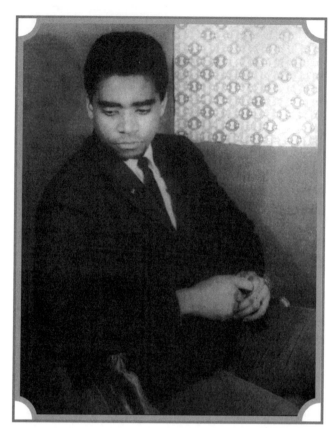

Opera star George Shirley in 1961.

Opera Stars

Camilla Williams was born on October 18, 1925 and began singing as a child in the choir of Danville's Calvary Baptist Church. With the help of a local music teacher, Williams studied voice and piano at Virginia State College and graduated with honors in 1941. She went on to teach but longed for a singing career. Camilla Williams won scholarships from black soprano Marian Anderson, who herself had made history when she was barred by the DAR from performing in Washington, D.C. Williams moved to Philadelphia for advanced voice study. She got her big break in 1946 when she was heard by opera singer Geraldine Farrar. Farrar became her mentor and Williams went on to debut with the New York City Opera later that year. In 1954 Williams made her debut with the Vienna Opera. Then in 1955

Marian Anderson became the first black to sing at New York's Metropolitan Opera. Robert McFerrin followed Marian Anderson as the second African-American to sing at the Metropolitan Opera in 1955, and George Shirley was the first African-American tenor to perform leading roles there. In 1969 black soprano Jessye Norman made her operatic debut at the Berlin Deutsche Opera. Other African-American opera stars include Leontyne Price, La Julia Rhea, Grace Bumbry, Shirley Verrett, Barbara Hendricks, Leona Mitchell, Harolyn Blackwell, Wilhelminia Fernandez, Marvis Martin, Clamma Dale, Isola Jones, Carmen Balthrop, Cynthia Clarey, and Kathleen Battle.

Jesse Owens

As a member of the United States track team at the 1936 Berlin Olympics, Jesse Owens earned four gold medals, but German leader Adolf Hitler refused to present them because he was black. "The Ebony Antelope" was born in Alabama in 1913 and made history competing in the collegiate Big Ten Championships in 1935. In 1955 President Dwight Eisenhower named Owens "Ambassador of Sports" and in 1976 he was awarded a Presidential Medal of Freedom. Owen's victories brought him fame and con-

Jesse Owens as a star at Ohio State.

tributed to the integration of American sports.

Pan-African Congress

W. E. B. Du Bois organized the Pan-African Congress to bring together Africans and leaders of nations involved in the African diaspora, and to promote the cause of African independence. He insisted that the conference be held in Paris in 1919 during the proceedings of the Paris Peace Conference. The second Pan-African Congress was held in 1921 in London, Brussels, and Paris; a third congress was held in 1923 in London and Lisbon; a fourth in New York City in 1927; and a fifth in Manchester, England, in 1945. The sixth Pan-African Congress was held in Dar es Salaam, Tanzania, in 1974. To keep African solidarity alive, Du Bois convened several subsequent gatherings.

Rosa Parks

In 1999, Rosa Parks, best know for her refusal to give up her seat in a public bus to a white man in 1955, was awarded the Congressional Medal of Honor and called "an icon for freedom in America." The bus incident occurred in Montgomery Alabama during early days of the Civil Rights Movement. Parks attended Alabama State College and worked for the Montgomery Voters League and the Youth Council of the

Rosa Park at her arrest in 1955.

NAACP. It was in her role as secretary of the NAACP that she made her stand on bus and helped to organize the Montgomery Bus Boycott. She has remained active in working for civil rights, receiving the NAACP's Spingarn Medal in 1970 and the Martin Luther King Award in 1980 in addition to her congressional medal.

Poll Tax

Prior to 1964, a poll tax was imposed on Southern voters as a pre-requisite for voting. This tax deprived many African-American and poor white voters from participating in elections. In 1964, the twenty-fourth amendment to the United States Constitution forbade the use of a poll tax in federal elections. In 1966, the Supreme Court extended the ruling to all elections, and the poll tax was abolished.

Poor People's Campaign

The Poor People's Campaign was initiated by Martin Luther King, Jr. in 1967 and was designed to recruit the poor of all races and backgrounds, train them in non-violent techniques and lead them in a protest designed to fight for greater economic rights. They were supposed to march on Washington, D.C. to begin a series of marches, sit-ins, rallies and boycotts designed to disrupt the government so that they would pass anti-poverty legislation. This movement was never fully realized. It ended with King's assassination on April 4th, 1968.

Gabriel Posser

Gabriel Prosser was born in Richmond, Virginia around 1776 and is credited with having plotted the first major slave revolt in United States history. His intention was to create a free black state in Virginia. His group of armed rebel slaves numbered more than 1,000. Their intent was to seize the arsenal at Richmond and kill the white people there. On August 30, 1800, the armed slaves gathered outside Richmond waiting to spring into action. An unexpected electrical rainstorm washed out the bridge that the rebels were planning to take to cross into the city. James Monroe, Virginia's Governor at the time, learned about the impending revolt and sent the state militia to deal with the slaves. The revolt failed and 35 slaves, including Gabriel Prosser, were hanged.

Post-emancipation Interviews

Post-emancipation interviews were a type of slave narrative that appeared after the Proclamation in 1863. Volunteer or paid employees of the federal government conducted interviews of former slaves–funded by two different federal programs, implemented decades apart. Immediately following the Civil War (starting in the late 1860s), many states' Freedmen's Bureaus conducted interviews of former slaves. During the 1930s, interviews were conducted as part of the Federal Writers' Project (FWP), for the Works Progress Administration (WPA), part of President Franklin D. Roosevelt's New Deal.

Colin L. Powell

In 1989, Powell, a four-star general in the Army, was chosen chairman of the Joint Chiefs of Staff. He was the youngest person and first African-American to hold the nation's highest military post. Powell was a career officer in United States Army, beginning in 1958. He served in the Vietnam War and Korea. He was Assistant to the Secretary of Defense, and a member of National Security Council. Powell helped plan the Persian Gulf War strategy during 1990 and 1991. He won a Spingarn Medal in 1991.

Mike Powell

Mike Powell won the 1988 Olympic Silver Medal for the long jump. In 1991, he outdid Carl Lewis at the World Track and Field Championship in Tokyo and broke Bob Beamon's long standing world record. Powell won the 1991 James E. Sullivan Trophy.

Presidential Cabinet Members

The first African-American member of a presidential Cabinet was Robert C. Weaver, secretary of Housing and Urban Development (HUD) (1966), and the second was William T. Coleman, Jr., Transportation (1975). Another secretary of HUD, Patricia Roberts Harris, was the first black woman in the Cabinet (1977). Andrew Young was named ambassador to the United Nations (1977). Clifford L. Alexander, Jr., became secretary of the Army (1977). In 1989 Louis W. Sullivan of Georgia was named secretary of Health and Human Services.

Leontyne Price

Leontyne Price was the first African-American woman to perform with the Metropolitan Opera, singing the role of Leonora in *Il Trovatore* in 1961. Price starred in a revival of *Porgy and Bess* (1952-54), and appeared at Vienna Opera and at La Scala in Milan. Born in 1927, she received a scholarship in 1949 to attend the Julliard School of Music. Price performed on Broadway before she made her Metropolitan Opera debut. Her vocal performances are known worldwide. Price was one of the first dozen artists honored with National Medal of Arts in 1985.

Leontyne Price performing in 1953.

Pulitzer Prizes

The poet Gwendolyn Brooks was the first black to win a Pulitzer Prize, for *Annie Allen* in 1950. *The Color Purple*, a best-selling novel by Alice Walker, won in 1983. Toni Morrison's novel *Beloved* took the prize in 1988. *A Soldier's Play* brought a Pulitzer for drama to Charles Fuller in 1982. Playwright August Wilson was a two-time Pulitzer prizewinner–for *Fences* (1987) and for *The Piano Lesson* (1990).

PUSH

PUSH is the acronym for People United to Save Humanity. It was a political organization designed by the Reverend Jesse Jackson in 1971. It used well-publicized boycotts to bring attention to and attain jobs and money from programs and organizations that discriminated against African-Americans. PUSH was also instrumental in blazing the trail of educational programs for African-American children.

Dudley (Felker) Randall

In 1965, Randall published a broadside (a publication printed on a single sheet of paper) of his poem "Ballad of Birmingham," about the 1963 race-motivated bombing of a Birmingham church where four little girls were attending Sunday school. With that initial publication, he founded Broadside Press. Broadside also played a crucial role in the development of the Black Arts Movement of the late 1960s and early

1970s, publishing the works of other poets, including Gwendolyn Brooks, Nikki Giovanni, Etheridge Knight, Audre Lorde, Haki Madhubuti (Don L. Lee), and Sonia Sanchez. Two other works by Randall are currently in print: *Black Poets* (1985), an anthology, and *Homage to Hoyt Fuller* (1984).

A. (Asa) Philip Randolph

In 1917, Randolph co-founded the outspokenly radical monthly magazine the *Messenger* (with Chandler Owen, who left the *Messenger* in 1923). The *Messenger* unflinchingly denounced leaders in the African-American community (e.g., Booker T. Washington, for his accommodationism; Marcus Garvey for his separatism; and W. E. B. Du Bois, for his failure to recognize the importance of class struggle). Randolph also attacked job and housing discrimination, railed against lynching, condemned African-American participation in World War I, and generally provoked the U.S. Justice Department to call him "the most dangerous Negro in America" in 1919. The *Messenger* was called "the most able and the most dangerous of all Negro publications." Despite the best efforts of the government, however, Randolph continued delivering his message month after month, year after year.

Randolph also took up the cause of the Pullman porters who worked for the railroads, leading them to found the Brotherhood of Sleeping Car Porters in 1925. Through the 1930s, the 1940s, the 1950s, and the 1960s, A. Philip Randolph was always in the lead, championing the rights of hard-working folks to earn a decent wage, without suffering discrimination, and with full civil rights.

Rap Music

Rap music is a musical form distinguished by spoken lyrics set to syncopated rhythms. The most popular rap singers were Hammer and L.L. Cool J.

Reconstruction Act of 1867

The Reconstruction Act of 1867 established five military districts in the South and gave all authority to the federal army.

Reconstruction and Post-Reconstruction

Reconstruction was the era between 1865 to 1877 following the Civil War. During this time, the states of the Confederacy were dominated by the federal government and later readmitted to the Union. The period of Reconstruction officially ended in 1877 when all federal troops were removed from the south. The Reconstruction period was one of disappointment and frustration for black people. After the Civil War, the freedmen were thrown largely on their own meager resources. Landless and uprooted, they moved about in search of work. The Southern states enacted laws resembling the slave codes of slave times. These laws restricted the movement of the former slaves in an effort to force them to work as plantation laborers—often for their former masters—at absurdly low wages. The federal Freedmen's Bureau, established by Congress in 1865, assisted the former slaves by giving them food and finding jobs and homes for them. The bureau established hospitals and schools, including such institutions of higher learning as Fisk University and Hampton Institute. Northern philanthropic agencies, such as the American Missionary Association, also aided the freedmen. During the Reconstruction period, blacks wielded political power in the South for the first time. Their leaders were largely clergymen, lawyers, and teachers who had been educated in the

North and abroad. Between 1869 and 1901, 20 black representatives and 2 black senators sat in the United States Congress. But Northern politicians grew increasingly conciliatory to the white South, so that by 1872 virtually all leaders of the Confederacy had been pardoned and were able to vote and hold office. Through economic pressure

and the terrorist activities of violent groups such as the Ku Klux Klan, most blacks were kept away from the polls. By 1877, with the withdrawal of the last federal troops from the South, Southern whites were again in full control. Only a few Southern black elected officials lingered on. No black was to serve in the United States Congress for three decades after 1901. States passed Jim Crow laws segregating blacks and whites in almost all public places. In the post-Reconstruction years, blacks received only a small share of the increasing number of industrial jobs in Southern cities. And relatively few rural blacks in the South owned their own farms, most remaining poor sharecroppers heavily in debt to white landlords. The largely urban Northern blacks fared little better. The jobs they sought were given to white European immigrants.

During and after the Reconstruction period, blacks in the cities organized historical, literary, and musical societies. The literary and musical achievements of African-Americans began to make a major impact on American mass culture.

Revolutionaries

During the 1960s militant black nationalist and Marxist-oriented black organizations were created, among them the Revolutionary Action Movement, the Deacons for Defense, and the Black Panther party. Under such leaders as Stokely Carmichael and H. Rap Brown SNCC adopted more radical policies. Some of the militant black leaders were arrested and others fled the country, seriously weakening their organizations.

The Rodney King Riots

The riots became the worst urban crisis of 20th century. On March 3, 1991, an African-American motorist, Rodney King, led police on a high-speed chase north of Los Angeles. When the car was stopped King resisted arrest. In subduing him, four white policemen administered a beating. This incident was caught on videotape by a witness, and the tape was replayed frequently to television audiences across the nation. The white policemen were brought to trial and the jury acquitted them of assault charges on April 29, 1992. In reaction, more than two days of looting, arson, assault, and killing broke out in south-central Los Angeles. When it was over 49 people were killed and about 1,400 were injured. Whole neighborhoods had been wiped out and thousands of jobs lost. Rioting and assorted violent incidents also occurred in other cities. In 1993 two of the police officers were convicted in federal court of violating King's civil rights.

The 1960s Riots

The riots of the 1960s involved fighting and the looting and burning of white-owned property in African-American ghettos across the nation. Hundreds of lives were lost, and tens of millions of dollars' worth of property were destroyed. Their basic causes were long-standing grievances–police insensitivity and brutality, inadequate educational and recreational facilities, high unemployment, poor housing, high prices. The fighting that took place was mainly between African-American youths and the police. The most serious disturbances occurred in the Watts area of Los Angeles, Calif., in July 1965 and in Newark and Detroit in July 1967. Anger and frustration over Martin Luther King's assassination in 1968, by a white drifter, set off more disturbances in the inner cities.

Paul Robeson

Born in Princeton, N.J., on April 9, 1898, Paul Robeson was the son of a runaway slave who became a minister. Robeson won a four-year scholarship to Rutgers, where he was the only black student and graduated as valedictorian of his class. He was outstanding at athletics, but chose academics over sports in the end, earning a law degree from Columbia Law School in 1923. During his first job at a law firm, however, he realized that the legal profession in 1923 would never allow a black American to reach his fullest potential. After facing a great deal of discrimination from employees who refused to work under an African-American, he decided to leave the law firm less than a year after starting work there.

His theatrical debut in 1921 impressed Eugene O'Neill, who created two powerful roles for him–Brutus Jones in *The Emperor Jones* and Jim in *All God's Chillun Got Wings*, a controversial play about interracial marriage. His performance of *Othello* was the longest recorded run of a Shakespearean play on Broadway. Robeson first sang his signature "Ol' Man River" in *Show Boat* in London in 1928. He made extended concert tours, and while touring in Europe, he was introduced to leftist views, and their emphasis on justice and racial and economic equality immediately appealed to him. During the McCarthy era his passport was revoked (1950-58) because he refused to renounce his beliefs in the principles of communism. He was blacklisted by concert managers, and his income plummeted, falling from $104,000 in 1947 to $2,000 afterward. When he published his autobiography, *Here I Stand* (1958), the *New York Times* and prominent literary journals not only refused to review it, but even refused to put it on their lists of new books.

During the course of his life, Robeson was a scholar, an all-American football player, a lawyer, a singer, an actor, and an author. He did all of these with tremendous grace and skill but it was his acting that earned him international fame. He was cut down at the height of his career during the beginning of the Cold War. It was a fall from which he never recovered. As his health failed, he remained in the United States, cut off from audiences and friends, and he refused even to attend tributes organized in his honor. He died in 1976 after suffering a stroke.

Paul Robeson as "Othello" in 1944.

Jackie Robinson

The whites-only barrier in major league baseball was broken when Jackie Robinson signed a contract with the Brooklyn Dodgers in 1947. He was one of many players in Negro Leagues baseball, and was followed into the majors by such greats as Satchel Paige, Monte Irvin, Larry Doby and Willie Mays.

Jackie Robinson signed on as a Brooklyn Dodger in 1947.

Frances A. (née) Rollin (Whipper)

Rollins' thoughts, her experiences, and her opinion exist in the oldest surviving diary by a southern African-American woman. She did her writing in the mid-1800s.

Moses Roper

Roper's *A Narrative of the Adventures and Escape of Moses Roper, from American Slavery* (1837) was one of the first such narratives by an African-American to appear in print. Roper's chronicle vividly documents the brutal treatment of slaves across the American Southeast before he escaped North to New England and then to England in 1835 (where slavery had been abolished in 1833), with the aid of American abolitionists.

Robinson Roscoe, Jr.

Roscoe was chosen by President Ronald Reagan as United States representative to the North Atlantic Treaty Organization (NATO) Military Committee (1982-85). He was the first African-American to become a four-star general in the Army. He was decorated in both the Korean and Vietnam wars.

Roots

Roots was one of television's most-watched dramatic telecasts. The eight-part miniseries was first shown in 1977. A sequel, the seven-part *Roots: The Next Generations*, appeared in 1979. Based on Alex Haley's novel, which was real-life search for his African ancestry, the shows made other African-Americans more aware of their rich cultural heritage.

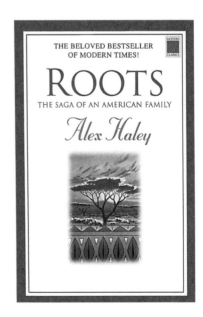

THE BELOVED BESTSELLER OF MODERN TIMES!

ROOTS
THE SAGA OF AN AMERICAN FAMILY
Alex Haley

Diana Ross

Born into a poor family in Detroit, Michigan in 1944, Diana Ross formed a singing group called the Primettes with two high school friends, and signed a recording contract with Motown in 1961, changing their name to the Supremes. During the 1960s, the Supremes had ten songs that reached number one on the *Billboard* charts, including "Baby Love," "Stop in the Name of Love," and "You Can't Hurry Love." Diana Ross started a solo career in 1970 that has included hit songs and lead roles in movies such as *Lady Sings the Blues*, *Mahogany*, and the *Wiz*.

Carl T. (Thomas) Rowan

Rowan became one of the first few African-American reporters to be employed by a major urban daily newspaper, the *Minneapolis Tribune*. A 1951 series of articles about the realities of the Jim Crow South earned Rowan a 1952 Sidney Hillman Award for the best newspaper reporting in the nation. A Rowan series about the historic 1954 Brown v. Board of Education of Topeka Supreme Court decision gained Rowan a 1954 Sigma Delta Chi Journalism Award from the Society of Professional Journalists, for the best general reporting. During the 1955 Montgomery bus boycott led by Martin Luther King, Jr., Rowan was the only African-American reporter covering the story for a national newspaper. Rowan won two more Sigma Delta Chi awards (for foreign correspondence) and was invited to become the first African-American member of the Gridiron Club, an organization of Washington, D.C., journalists (founded in 1885). In 1961, Rowan accepted appointments in the Kennedy and then the Johnson administrations. He made top-secret negotiations with the Soviet Union to free U.S. pilot Francis Gary Powers, whose U2 spy plane had been shot down over the USSR. He also became not only the first African-American to serve on the National Security Council (NSC) but also the first ever to attend an NSC meeting. In 1963, Rowan was appointed the ambassador to Finland, thereby becoming the youngest ambassador and only the fifth African-American ever to serve as an envoy. In 1964, President Johnson asked Rowan to become the director of the United States Information Agency (USIA). Again, he broke ground as the first African-American to lead this important post and was then the highest-ranking African-American ever to serve in the State Department. Rowan went on to write nationally syndicated columns, and made regular appearances as a broadcaster and guest on radio and television programs. Rowan wrote several books, including *Breaking Barriers: A Memoir* (1991); and *The Coming Race War in America: A Wake-Up Call* (1996). He died in September 2000.

Royal African Company of 1672

In North America, the English chartered companies had a colonizing as well as a trading purpose. The Hudson's Bay Company was mostly devoted to trade. The London Company, the Plymouth Company, and the Massachusetts Bay Company were involved in the settlement of colonists. Other chartered English companies were set up for the development of new trade. The Canary Company in 1665 and the South Sea Company in 1711 were short lived. In 1663 England chartered the company of Royal Adventurers which was renamed the Royal African Company in 1672. It officially earmarked blacks as commodities, or chattel, to be exchanged across the Middle Passage in the slave trade. The Royal African Company was set up so British colonies could obtain African slaves directly from British traders. It had a monopoly on slaving. It transported 70,000 slaves yearly until 1698. In that year, all Englishmen were granted the right to trade in slaves. By 1750 a new company, Merchants Trading to Africa, dealt in slaves through ports in London, Bristol, and Liverpool.

David Ruggles

Born free, of free parents, in a free state (Connecticut), Ruggles had passionate feelings against slavery. When he was just 20 years old, he wrote a letter to the French Marquis de Lafayette, asking him to help abolish slavery. Ruggles was a regular contributor to the *Emancipator* and the *Liberator*, and in 1833, Ruggles worked as an agent lecturing for the *Emancipator*, drumming up business for the abolitionist newspaper and stirring his listeners to oppose slavery. The next year (1834), in New York City, he opened the first known African-American bookshop, where he sold abolitionist pamphlets (some of which he authored) and other materials. He also founded the New York Committee for Vigilance, putting his beliefs into action. The committee worked with the Underground Railroad, using its members as interference between slave catchers and fugitive slaves. In this way, Ruggles risked his own life and well being to protect more than a thousand fugitive slaves, including Frederick Douglass. In 1838, he started publishing the committee's *Mirror of Liberty*, perhaps the nation's first African-American weekly magazine. Ruggles also published a *New York Slaveholders Directory* (1839), unmasking whites who were thought to have captured and enslaved free men and women.

Bill Russell

Born in Louisiana in 1934, Russell attended the University of San Francisco on a basketball scholarship and led his college team to the NCAA championship in 1955 and 1956. When he played at the 1956 Olympic Games in Melbourne, Australia, the United States team won a gold medal. Russell joined the Boston Celtics in 1957, where he was named Most Valuable Player five times and helped the Celtics becomes one of the most successful teams in professional sports. An outspoken advocate of equal rights for African-American athletes, he became the first African-American head coach in the NBA.

Bayard Rustin

A protégé of A. Philip Randolph, Rustin wrote numerous essays (many of which were collected in *Down the Line: The Collected Writings of Bayard*

Rustin, 1971) and published *Strategies for Freedom: The Changing Patterns of Black Protest* (1976). He also ghostwrote many of the civil-rights writings and speeches by and about Martin Luther King, Jr., and he kept a journal of his thoughts and experiences.

Sonia Sanchez
(née Wilsonia Driver)

A prolific writer, Sanchez sometimes functions as a prophet when she calls for justice and equality for all peoples of the world. At other times, she writes passionately of love and intimate relationships. Ultimately, her powerful language and her universal messages has made her one of the most significant African-American writers to emerge from the Black Arts Movement.

Sanchez began her academic career in 1965 at the Downtown Community School in San Francisco. She then taught at San Francisco State College (1967-1969), where she helped establish the first Black Studies program in the United States. During these years, Sanchez became politically active in the Congress of Racial Equality (CORE) and the Nation of Islam (1972-1975). After several posts at various colleges and universities, Sanchez settled in Philadelphia at Temple University in 1977. She remains on the faculty there, teaching and maintaining a schedule of national and international readings of her work.

Sanchez has published more than 10 books of poetry including *home coming*, (1969); *We are a Baddddd People* (1970); *Blues Book for Blue Black Magical Women* (1974); *homegirls & handgrenades* (1984); *I've Been a Woman: New and Selected Poems* (1985); *Wounded in the House of a Friend* (1995); and *Like the Singing Coming off*

the Drums (1998). She has also published six plays and three children's books: *It's a New Day: Poems for Young Brothas and Sistuhs* (1971); *The Adventures of Flathead, Smallhead, and Squarehead* (1973); and *A Sound Investment: Short Stories for Young Readers* (1980). Sanchez also edited two books, and her work has been anthologized in numerous books and published in many journals and magazines. She has also garnered several important academic distinctions and literary awards, notably the 1985 American Book Award for *homegirls & handgrenades*.

Carrie Saxon-Perry

Carrie Saxon Perry was born in Hartford Connecticut in 1931. She served as an administrator in various Hartford organizations including the Welfare Department. From 1981 to 1987, she was a representative in the Connecticut General Assembly. In 1987, Saxon Perry was elected mayor of Hartford and reelected in 1989. She was the first black woman to be elected mayor of a large city.

Schomburg, Arthur A.
(né Arturo Alfonso Schomburg)

Essentially, Arthur Schomburg dedicated his life to demonstrating the long, rich history of Africans, both in Africa and in the Americas, and to showing the countless profoundly important contributions of persons of African descent across the world.

In 1911 Schomburg and Edward Bruce cofounded the Negro Society for Historical Research. The society (of which Schomburg was secretary-treasurer and librarian for many years) was dedicated to publishing articles on African-American history, based on research conducted by society members. Participation in these groups encouraged Schomburg to be more rigorous and systematic in his own collection of books and other artifacts.

In 1914, Schomburg was invited to join the American Negro Academy (ANA), which Alexander Crummell had founded in 1879. Fellow members included W. E. B. Du Bois, Alain Locke, Kelly Miller,

Carter G. Woodson, and numerous other scholars. This association helped him further refine his bibliophilic research skills and encouraged his abiding dedication to research in African-American culture and history. Over time, Schomburg amassed a broad well-organized, prodigious collection of literary works and visual artworks by persons of African descent. He had also become well known for his sophisticated ability to recognize choice items and to find rare or missing materials. In 1926, the New York Public Library (NYPL) opened its Division of Negro Literature, History, and Prints at its 135th Street (off of Lenox Avenue in Harlem) branch, based largely on the purchase of Schomburg's private collection. Schomburg's collection itself also offered a tremendous resource to writers and other artists of the Harlem Renaissance and of every era since. At some point, the collection was renamed the Schomburg Collection of Negro Literature and History and still later was renamed the Schomburg Center for Research in Black Culture. Many researchers acknowledge the center as the world's largest and most important repository of materials on African and African-American history and culture, now including more than 5 million items.

Dred Scott

Dred Scott was a slave who had been purchased in 1832, and taken to Illinois and the Wisconsin territory at a time when slavery was prohibited in those lands by the Missouri Compromise. Scott was brought back to St. Louis, Missouri. When his master died in 1843, Scott sued for his freedom on the basis that he lived in a free state and territory. Eventually the case reached the Supreme Court. The Dred Scott Case in 1856-1857 involved the status of slavery in the federal territories. Scott lost the case but was freed a few weeks later. He died in 1858.

Dred Scott sued for his freedom.

Secession

The breaking away of 11 Southern states from the Union in 1860-1861, hastened the Civil War. South Carolina was an advocate of states' rights and became the first state to secede from the Union. in 1861.

Betty Shabazz

Hajj Bahiyah Betty Shabazz, American educator and widow of black leader Malcolm X, became an international African-American icon. She had attended Tuskegee University, then moved to New York City and studied at the Brooklyn State Hospital School of Nursing. During her junior year, she attended the Nation of Islam's Temple No. 7 in Harlem. There she taught a women's health class and was noticed by Malcolm X, who was a minister at the temple. They were married in 1958. They became the parents of six daughters. Shabazz was pregnant when Malcolm was assassinated in the Audubon Ballroom in New York City on February 21, 1965. She and her other children witnessed the event.

After Malcolm's death, Shabazz raised her children and continued her education, which culminated in a Ph.D. degree in educational administration from the University of Massachusetts. She taught health sciences and then became head of public relations at Medgar Evers College in Brooklyn. She left the Nation of Islam at the time of Malcolm's death, but took the hajj, the sacred Islamic pilgrimage to Mecca, in Saudi Arabia. She believed that Malcolm had been murdered by the Nation of Islam, but in 1995 made a public reconciliation with Louis Farrakhan, the head of the Nation of Islam. Her reconciliation with Farrakhan helped to establish his legitimacy in the African-American community.

Shabazz's presence aided even more in the rehabilitation of Malcolm X himself. Betty Shabazz's kept Malcolm's name and message fresh. She was active in African-American social organizations such as the Links, Delta Sigma Theta, and Jack and Jill of America. On June 1, 1997, Betty Shabazz's only grandson, 12-year-old Malcolm Shabazz, set fire to her apartment in Yonkers, New York. A troubled child, he was staying with his grandmother because his own mother, Qubilah, had problems of her own, including substance abuse and involvement in a plot to kill Farrakhan. In the fire, Shabazz received third-degree burns over 95 percent of her body, and she died three weeks later.

Assata Olugbala Shakur
(née JoAnne Deborah Byron; married name: Chesimard)

In her book, *Assata: An Autobiography* (1987), Shakur candidly (and often with good humor) described her formative years, as well as her experiences as an activist in the Black Panther Party in the early and mid-1970s. She was a questionably convicted accomplice to the murder of a white state trooper in 1977, a prisoner, and an escaped prisoner residing with political asylum in Cuba (since 1979).

Noble Sissle

Sissle was the primary lyricist to collaborate with noted pianist and composer Eubie Blake. Their ground-breaking 1921 show, *Shuffle Along*, one of the first musicals to be written, directed, and produced by African-Americans, as well as performed by blacks. Their song "I'm Just Wild about Harry" was popular for years.

1712 Slave Act

In 1712, a slave revolt threatened to demolish New York City. The group of rebels consisted of about twenty to thirty African-American slaves and two Indians. They set fire to a building and attacked several whites who came to put out the blaze. The event led to the death of nine whites with others wounded. Ultimately the rebellion was ended and most of the rebels were seized. As a result, twenty-one slaves were executed after a trial. New York passed the 1712

Slave Act in an effort to suppress uprisings. Massachusetts constructed a law against further importation of slaves into that colony, and Pennsylvania set high taxes to keep Africans out.

Ntozake Shange
(née Paulette Williams)

Shange developed a distinctive artistic form, which she calls a "choreopoem." These verse narratives, which are presented on stage, are accompanied by music and dance. Her first finished choreopoem was *for colored girls who have considered suicide / when the rainbow is enuf* (published in 1976). In this choreopoem, seven African-American women act, sing, dance, and recite 20 poems. Her choreopoem was performed on Broadway (only the second play by an African-American woman to reach Broadway) for two years in the mid-1970s, winning an Obie Award, as well as Emmy, Tony (for best play), and Grammy Award nominations. The play also earned Outer

Critics Circle, Audelco, and *Mademoiselle* awards and was chosen for international performances. Additional plays by Shange include her 1981 Obie Award-winning *Mother Courage and Her Children* (1980). In addition to her plays, Shange has written several novels including *Betsey Brown* (1985), a semi-autobiographical novel set in the late 1950s, when the author and the civil-rights movement were coming of age; and *Liliane: Resurrection of the Daughter* (1994), about the psychological development of a wealthy African-American woman living in the South. Shange's free-verse highlights the African-American oral tradition through nonconformist syntax, capitalization, spelling, and idiomatic vocabulary and language structure.

Sharecropping
(or tenant farming)

Sharecropping is a farm tenancy system that was widespread in the southern regions of the United

States after the Civil War. At the close of the War, the southern plantation system began to change. Former slaves needed to provide for themselves. Landowners made farming land, seed, and credit available to the croppers who would work the land in return for a share of the yield. The croppers received a share of the value of the crops less the amount of money owed to the landlord for their expenses. Landlords abused the system by demanding more and more from the croppers. High interest charges made it impossible for the croppers to keep up with the debts incurred. The focus on a single cash crop also encumbered the system. The New Deal farm programs of the Roosevelt era eventually brought about the eviction of thousands of southern sharecroppers.

Ann (née Ann Allen) Shockley

One of the leading university archivists of African-American women's writing, Shockley's first book-length projects were outstanding reference works, used by fellow archivists. Her early work ranges from a thorough description of the inadequacies of segregated public-library services in the Jim Crow South to a biographical directory describing numerous African-American writers and a handbook that specifically tells librarians how to gather and protect materials on African-American history. In addition, Shockley has written articles and has edited volumes about various issues including oral history, literacy, and racism in children's literature. Shockley's nonfiction work has wide appeal: *Afro-American Women Writers (1746-1933): An Anthology and Critical Guide* (1988), which places more than 40 writers in their historical and cultural context. Shockley has also written fiction. Her 1974 novel *Loving Her* focuses on an interracial lesbian love affair, and her second novel, *Say Jesus and Come to Me* (1982) addresses the issue of homophobia in the African-American church. A collection of short stories, *The Black and White of It* (1980) includes, "A Meeting of the Sapphic Daughters" revealing racism in the women's movement.

Slave Narratives

Slave narratives are the recordings and recollections of slaves and former slaves. Slave narratives enable us to trace over 300 years of history in which millions of people were brought to the United States, literally in chains. The narratives provide distinctive insight into the everyday experiences of slaves and former slaves, from the earliest days of fifteenth- and sixteenth-century slave trading in Africa through the postemancipation period. Without such narratives, these experiences would be invisible to most readers of traditional history books.

The narratives also offer distinctive insight into particular aspects of U.S. history. For instance, many of these narratives show how Southern plantations underwent historical changes. In the early years, most of these plantations were relatively small, independent farms with a few slaves, located mainly in the coastal colonies of Virginia and the Carolinas. Over time, however, the plantations grew to large, complex slave-holding homesteads, which spread from the coastal colonies through the southern colonies and states to Texas.

Slave narratives may be sorted into three types, based on the origin of the account: (1) authentic narratives, written directly by slaves, in their own words, during or soon after their enslavement; (2) narratives recorded by amanuenses (people who wrote down what others dictated) during or soon after the narrator's enslavement, which were often heavily edited by the amanuenses; or (3) narratives recorded after slavery had officially ended (in 1863), based on interviews between former slaves and government workers. Clearly, the credibility and reliability of the account varies across these three basic forms. Therefore, readers need to know which type of account they are reading in order to know how readily to believe the account.

Slavery

During a period that spanned some 240 years (1619-1859), African slaves were ferried across the Atlantic to an unsettling future of forced servitude

in North America. This led to profitable slave trade carried out by the British, French, Dutch, Spanish, and Portuguese. The discovery of America created enormous growth in the economies of the world. The Atlantic trade route known as the Triangular trade route between Africa, the West Indies, and America brought about prosperity the world had never known. The toll on the African continent, however, was devastating to most of its peoples. The total number of slaves brought to the West was approximately 11 mil-

lion. Millions more were either killed in the quest for their capture, or taken to Europe or the Middle East to be sold into slavery. The logs from one ship indicated that nearly half of its cargo of slaves had died as the result of dysentery. Slaves who were found to be sick were often thrown overboard to avoid widespread contamination. Goods were transported from British ports for the West Coast of Africa. There they were exchanged for African slaves who were taken to the New World and traded for agricultural staples for the return to England.

James Webster Smith

James Webster Smith of South Carolina was one of the first African-Americans to become a cadet at West Point in 1870. While he did not graduate, Smith did go on to train cadets at South Carolina State College.

Soul Music

Soul Music is the first style of distinctly African-American popular music. During the 1950s, the popularity of black performers such as Nat "King" Cole, Dinah Washington, Chuck Berry, and the Platters revealed the beginnings of integration in American pop music. Soul emerged in the 1960s from rhythm-and-blues and gospel. Classic soul artists include James Brown, Sam Cooke, Ray Charles, Isaac Hayes, Marvin Gaye, Arlene Smith and the Chantels, and Jerry Butler and The Impressions. Many elements of the style are evident in Gladys Knight and the Pips. There was the harder-edged "Memphis sound," associated with Stax Records (1960-1975) of Memphis, Tennessee, and the slicker, more pop-oriented "Motown sound," represented by Berry Gordy's Detroit-based Motown Records (founded in 1959). In addition, James Brown had a rhythmic and danceable style all his own. The hard soul of Stax, and of New York City's Atlantic Records, featured stripped-down production values and gritty small ensembles. Stax's Booker T. and the MGs and the Bar-Kays, provided a powerful rhythmic drive and tightly riffing horns behind the gospel-and blues-tinged vocals of such singers as Otis Redding, Sam Moore and David Prater, Carla Thomas, the Staple Singers, Wilson Pickett, and Aretha Franklin.

Gordy's Motown recordings employed a more lavish production, and achieved a sweeter sound that appealed to whites as well as blacks. Among Motown's most influential artists were Diana Ross and the Supremes, Smokey Robinson and the Miracles, Stevie Wonder, the Jackson Five, and the Temptations. But prior to the soul music era, black musicians had gained success primarily by appealing to the musical tastes of white listeners. Soul music also inspired a "white soul" counterpart, exemplified in the early 1970s by such white pop singers as Carole King and Van Morrison. Hayes, Curtis Mayfield, and Stevie Wonder in particular invested their music with a strong social conscience. Although some African-American artists, such as Donna Summer and the Commodores, had hits during the 1970s disco craze, African-American listeners preferred the harder-edged funk style.

Southern Christian Leadership Council

The Southern Christian Leadership Council (SCLC) was created to spread the Civil Rights Movement out from Montgomery and through the South as a whole. The movement's first goal was to

The Rev. Martin Luther King, Jr. founded the Southern Christian Leadership Council in 1957.

increase black voter registration in the South, which had been held back by various discriminatory laws that allowed for literacy tests and poll taxes that prevented many African-Americans from access to the voting booths. Their ultimate goal, of course, was the complete elimination of segregation.

Southern Plantations

The Southern Plantation system was based on the planting of crops such as cotton and tobacco. The crops were grown on estates or farms in the Southern subtropical climate and were at one time worked by African slave labor.

Southern Tenant Farmers Union

The Southern Tenant Farmers Union, also called The Green Rising, was comprised of black and white sharecroppers and their families who had become displaced and homeless when the sharecropping system failed. Founded by seven black and eleven white sharecroppers in Arkansas, the STFU was to become a strong force in the American Labor movement. The union eventually paved the way for the development of the La Follette Civil Liberties Committee in the United States Senate and the Kennedy-Johnson Administration's War on Poverty. It is also recognized as a model for the United Farm Worker's of America.

Spelman College

Spelman College in Atlanta, Georgia is the oldest black women's college in the United States. Two white New England missionaries, Sophia Packard and Harriet Giles, who were concerned about the lack of educational opportunities for Southern black women founded it. In 1881 the first classes of the Atlanta Baptist Female Seminary, as it was originally called, met in a church basement with 11 students. Three months later the enrollment had grown to 80, and within a year, 200 women ranging in age from 15 to 52 attended the school. Giles and Packard received donations from American industrialist John D. Rockefeller. The school was renamed Spelman Seminary after Rockefeller's wife Laura Spelman Rockefeller. In 1901 Spelman granted its first two college degrees. In 1924 the school officially changed its name to Spelman College. By 1930 its focus was solely on liberal arts education. In 1988 African American entertainer Bill Cosby and his wife Camille gave Spelman a widely publicized $20 million gift. In the 1990s Spelman received national attention for its role as a site of the 1996 Olympic Games in Atlanta and for its recognition as the best liberal arts college in the South by a leading poll of American colleges and universities. Spelman alumnae include Pulitzer Prize-winning author Alice Walker, attorney and children's rights advocate Marian Wright Edelman, and former Acting Surgeon General Audrey Manley. Nearly 2,000 women are currently enrolled at Spelman.

Spingarn, Arthur B. (Barnett); Spingarn, Joel Elias

Both Spingarn brothers (of European-American heritage) were heavily involved in the activities of the National Association for the Advancement of Colored People (NAACP): Arthur, an attorney, chaired the NAACP's legal committee for many years and served as the organization's president (1940-1965); Joel chaired the NAACP board in 1914, and at that time, he established the organization's prestigious Spingarn medal, awarded to outstanding African-Americans who have made significant contributions to their community in various fields of endeavor. Joel also encouraged many writers of the Harlem Renaissance and wrote such works of literary criticism as *A History of Literary Criticism in the Renaissance* (1899) and *The New Criticism* (1911). Those volumes serve as bookends to his career teaching literature at Columbia University from 1899 to1911. Spingarn also worked closely with Walter White, whom he had met when White had consulted with Spingarn about his first novel (in 1922), when Spingarn was an editor at Harcourt and Brace. The two were instrumental in shaping the NAACP's financial and administrative policies during the 1930s.

In 1946, Arthur Spingarn, a noted collector of literature by and about people of African descent (especially rare editions of Cuban, Haitian, and Brazilian authors), made his 5,000-plus books available to Howard University. Howard's president at the time, Mordecai Wyatt Johnson, observed that it was "the most comprehensive and interesting group of books by Negroes ever collected in the world." Even after Howard acquired his collection, Arthur Spingarn continued to send to Howard a copy of every book he could find, which was written by an author of African descent, including books on various academic topics, written in African and European languages. In recognition of his contribution, Howard named their world-renowned research center the Moorland-Spingarn Research Center in 1973.

Spirituals

African-American spirituals have been seen as the first indigenous music of the United States. In their mixture of sorrow and joy, spirituals paved the way for other genres of music such as blues and jazz. African-American religious songs are believed to have been sung since the days when Africans were brought to the New World as slaves. In 1801, Richard Allen gathered some of the spirituals into a book. By then, however, many spirituals had been lost because they had fallen out of use or had been modified through the generations. Spirituals probably emerged out of the contact between the traditions of the African slaves and the Protestant Christianity of the South, intent on spreading its religion to all races. Although African-American spirituals may have picked up the details of the Bible stories, evangelical sermons, and hymns from the Protestants, they are distinct from white religious songs because of the African influences that the slaves incorporated into their spirituals. The songs have long, repetitive choruses, employ call-and-response patterns of West and Central Africa (in which the lead singer sings a line and the rest of the congregation sing the same line or a responding line back), include percussion and syncopation (if not performed with instruments, singers would use their hands and feet to keep the beat), and encourage the congregation and singers to incorporate rhythmic body movements.

The Fisk Jubilee singers introduced traditional black spirituals to audiences around the world. They performed at the White House for President Chester A. Arthur in 1882.

In many ways the songs were as much about protest as spiritual redemption. While songs such as "Swing Low, Sweet Chariot" and "Go Down Moses" call for a spiritual liberation that is overtly religious, they also hint at an actual yearning for freedom that slaves were denied. So threatening were the words of these songs that slaveholders forbade slaves to sing some of them as they worked the plantations.

Sports

African-Americans have achieved remarkable success in sports and it has been the backdrop for major racial events in American history. Horse racing was one of the first sports in which African-Americans made their mark. By the mid-nineteenth century black jockeys dominated the profession. In the first 28 years of the Kentucky Derby, from 1875 to 1902, black jockeys won the race 15 times, including three victories by Isaac Murphy, the most celebrated jockey of the age. Blacks engaged in baseball as early as the 1860s, and numerous black teams flourished in local leagues. From the 1920s through the early 1940s, black organized baseball reached its peak with the success of the Negro Leagues. Football burst onto the scene in the 1890s at colleges and universities in the East and rapidly gained in popularity among African-Americans. African-American athletes such as William H. Lewis and William Tecumseh Sherman Jackson won early national acclaim in the sport. As a result of the efforts in the early twentieth century of organizations including the Colored Intercollegiate Athletic Association, track and field emerged as a popular organized athletic activity among African-Americans of all ages. The successes of the first African-American professional basketball team of note, the Harlem Renaissance Big Five, helped enormously to popularize the sport among all races. Tennis and golf were able to make modest inroads into the African-American world of sports, owing to the work in particular of two black athletic organizations: the American Tennis Association, and the United Golfers Association.

Despite the ideals of sportsmanship and fair play, however, African-Americans faced restrictions or were barred outright from participation in every avenue of sport. Blacks first made their marks in individualized athletics such as boxing, but not without overcoming tremendous racial obstacles. In team sports, the overwhelming majority of African-American athletes who competed prior to World War II, did so on all-black teams. Only a small number of white colleges and universities in the North allowed blacks to participate in their athletic programs. Integrated teams and interracial sporting competitions were against the law in many Southern states until as late as the 1950s.

Two black athletes dominated American sports in the years immediately prior to World War II: Jesse Owens in track and field and Joe Louis in boxing. Owens's four gold medals in the 1936 Olympic Games in Berlin, Germany, were seen as a triumph for American democracy over Nazism, as was Louis's defeat of German boxer Max Schmeling in their second heavyweight fight in 1938. Boxing great Henry Armstrong hammered away at discrimination in the 1930s and 1940s by refusing to fight in segregated arenas. Students at New York University launched a protest in 1940 against racial discrimination in collegiate athletics that gained national recognition and support to eradicate the color line in intercollegiate sports. America's entry into World War II had a strong impact on the color line in sports as the diversion of American manpower to the war effort left a vacuum in professional and amateur athletics that African Americans helped to fill. In this period, Satchel Paige and his Negro Baseball All-Star Team were given the opportunity to play the major league champions of baseball, and the Negro Collegiate All-Stars of Football played successive games against the champions of the National Football League. The number of African-American athletes in predominantly white collegiate conferences also increased.

The integration of sports continued after the war ended in 1945. In 1947 Jackie Robinson broke the color line to become the first black player in major league baseball. In professional basketball, Chuck Cooper and Sweetwater Clifton came into the National Basketball Association in 1950. That year also marked an important first in tennis when Althea Gibson became the first African-American woman to compete in the National Championships (later the United States Open) at Forest Hills in Queens, New York, an event she would later win in 1957 and 1958. In the 1960s Wilma Rudolph and Wyomia Tyus won international acclaim for African-American women in track. The brash personality of boxing champion Muhammad Ali and his defiant stand against military induction during the Vietnam War was a defining element of the 1960s. Despite its many barriers, sports stood as one of the early venues where blacks gained a foothold, and it remains one of the best-publicized routes to success for African-Americans. Nonetheless, it has led to a pervasive stereotype of black athletes as gifted in body but not in mind and has contributed to a belated acceptance of blacks as coaches and managers and in on-field leadership positions such as football quarterback. Only since the 1980s has sports witnessed the successes of such African-American coaches and managers as Cito Gaston and Dusty

Joe Louis triumphed over German boxer Max Schmeling in 1938.

Baker in baseball, Dennis Green in football, and Lenny Wilkens in basketball. Star football quarterbacks such as Doug Williams, Warren Moon, and Randall Cunningham, have also begun to break that stubborn barrier.

States' Rights

States' Rights was a statement of official government policy based on the tenth amendment to the Constitution. Its assertion was that "the powers not delegated to the United States by the Constitution, nor prohibited by it to the States, are reserved to the states respectively, or to the people." It was used by the pro-slavery states to justify secession. In the twentieth century, Southern opponents of the federal civil rights program revived states' rights.

Thaddeus Stevens

A United States Representative from Pennsylvania during 1849 to 1853 and 1859 until1868, Thaddeus Stevens is recognized for having led the radical republican reconstruction efforts after the Civil War. His program assisted the African-American claim to freedom by proposing the fourteenth amendment to the United States Constitution thereby guaranteeing civil rights for black people.

Maria W. (née Maria Miller) Stewart

In 1831, Stewart wrote "Religion and the Pure Principles of Morality, the Sure Foundation on Which We Must Build," using both the Bible and the U.S. Constitution as authorities for asserting a universal right to freedom, equality, and justice. Stewart urged African-Americans to organize resistance to slavery in the South and to oppose racist discrimination and restrictions in the North. William Lloyd Garrison, publisher of the Liberator, printed her manuscript as a pamphlet; thereafter, he published the texts of all her essays, speeches, and other writings. Stewart's second public speech made history: in 1832, she became the first American-born woman documented to have given a public lecture to a "promiscuous audience" (both men and women) on political topics.

Stewart's published works include her pamphlet "Meditations from the Pen of Mrs. Maria Stewart" (which she enlarged and published herself half a century later) and her 1835 "Productions of Mrs. Maria W. Stewart," a collection of speeches, biographical facts, and several poems and essays on topics including abolition, human rights, and women's rights to economic equality, education, and moral uplift. Whenever she spoke or wrote, Stewart exhorted well-off white women to sympathize with the plight of their darker-skinned brothers and sisters. She encouraged all women and African-American men to gain education, citing it as a source of uplift and urged all women to participate fully and equally in the political and social life of their communities.

William Still

In 1872, long after Emancipation and the close of the Civil War, Still published the first edition of his book, *The Underground Rail Road: a Record of Facts, Authentic Narratives, Letters, &C., Narrating the Hardships Hair-Breadth Escapes and Death Struggles of the Slaves in Their Efforts For Freedom, as Related by Themselves and Others, or Witnessed by the Author; Together with Sketches of Some of the Largest Stockholders, and Most Liberal Aiders and Advisers on the Road.* The text came from Still's journal of his activities with the Anti-Slavery Society. He had raised funds and disbursed them to conductors on the Underground Railroad, trained and coordinated the activities of the slavehunter lookouts, established safe houses, and found ways to provide forged free papers, food, clothing, medical care, jobs, money, and friends to fugitive slaves. He also provided contacts and resources for fugitives to escape farther north, to the safety of Canada. He and his wife, Letitia George Still, also opened their homes to fugitives. In various ways, Still managed to help about 800 people find their way to freedom.

After slavery ended, Still worked with various social and civic organizations, encouraging other people to donate whatever resources they had to their community. He helped to found an old folks home, an orphanage, and a YMCA. In 1888, Still and his son-in-law Matthew Anderson started the Berean Building and Loan Association, which enabled many Philadelphia families to buy property, including their own homes. Anderson was the second husband of Still's daughter Caroline Virginia Still Wiley Anderson, one of the first African-American women to graduate from a medical school (in 1878) and to practice medicine.

Carl Stokes

A lawyer, Carl Stoke's political career began in 1962 when he became the first African-American Democrat elected to the Ohio legislature. His next step was his election as mayor of Cleveland, the first African-American elected mayor of a major American city. Stokes retired from politics to become a journalist, becoming the first black news anchor in the New York City area in 1972, working for NBC television. He then returned to his legal career, becoming counsel to the United Auto Workers in Cleveland and then elected a municipal court judge. In 1994 President Bill Clinton made him an ambassadors to Seychelles in the Indian Ocean.

The Stono Rebellion

The Stono Rebellion was one of the earliest slave revolts in 1739. It led to the deaths of no less than 20 white people and more than 40 black people in the colony of South Carolina, west of Charleston.

"Stop the Terror"

Stop the Terror was an all-day summit sponsored by the Atlanta-based Center for Democratic Renewal

on March 26, 2000. Martin Luther King III, son of the civil rights leader, Reverend Martin Luther King, Jr., marched from downtown Atlanta to the King memorial. The summit and the march were part of a four day event promoted by the National Crime Prevention Council and Youth Crime Watch of America.

Harriet Beecher Stowe

Stowe's novel, *Uncle Tom's Cabin* (1852), was turned down by several publishers, and the publisher that finally accepted the work offered either to provide a 10% royalty or to share both the costs of the printing and the profits from the book's sales. European-American abolitionist Stowe unwisely chose the former option. The book sold 3,000 copies the first day out its initial printing of 5,000 copies in 2 days and half a million copies within 5 years. Later, on meeting her, Civil War President Abraham Lincoln said, "So you're the little woman who wrote the book that made this great war." She had based her novel on several slave narratives, such as those of Frederick Douglass and Josiah Henson. Henson subsequently claimed the

for African Methodism (1867), *The Negro's Origin, or Is He Cursed of God?* (1869), *The Color Solomon: What?* (1896), *The Negro in Holy Writ* (1898), and *A Hint to Ministers, Especially Those of the African Methodist Episcopal Church* (1900). Tanner also edited publications of the African Methodist Episcopal (A.M.E.) Church and founded and edited the quarterly A.M.E. *Church Review*, the first African-American scholarly journal.

Mildred (Delois) Taylor

When Mildred was just a few months old, her father had to flee from their home in Jackson, Mississippi, to avoid a violent confrontation with a white man. A few months later, his family joined him in Toledo, Ohio. Although her father left the South, he never left behind the rhythms and idioms of rural African-American Southern speech, the lifestyles and folkways of African-American Southern culture, and the Southern storytelling craft.

After earning a bachelor's in education (1965) at the University of Toledo, Taylor joined the Peace Corps, spending two years in Ethiopia teaching English and history. After her return, she earned her master's degree and spent several years teaching, but she left her job to write stories that would more accurately reflect African-American history.

Her novella *Song of the Trees* was published in 1975. This book introduces readers to the Logan family, which lived through slavery, Reconstruction, and the Jim Crow South. Her book's simple story, vividly appealing characters, and poetically authentic speech were critically acclaimed (named the *New York Times Outstanding Book of the Year*). Taylor's second book about the Logans was *Roll of Thunder, Hear My Cry* (1976), often cited as a contemporary classic of children's literature. Taylor has won a Newbery Medal, two Boston Globe-Horn Book Honor Book citations, a Buxtehude Bulle Award, a National Book Award nomination, two Coretta Scott King Awards, and an American Book Award nomination. In 1988, the Children's Interracial Book Council honored Taylor "for a body of work that has examined significant social issues and presented them in outstanding books for young readers."

title "Uncle Tom" and wrote two more narratives after Stowe's book was published. Many other African-American authors (e.g., Martin R. Delany, Frances Ellen Watkins Harper, and Paul Laurence Dunbar) have written works directly or indirectly referring to Stowe and her antislavery novel.

Benjamin Tucker Tanner

In addition to writing poems and journals, Tanner wrote several scholarly and theological books, including *Paul versus Pius Ninth* (1865), *An Apology*

Television Comedies

Redd Foxx and Demond Wilson starred in the popular *Sanford and Son* series in 1972-77. One of the most acclaimed weekly shows ever produced was *The Cosby Show* (1984-92). Its spin-off, *A Different World*, consistently ranked in the top ten prime-time shows. Keenan Ivory Wayans, star of the satirical comedy show *In Living Color*, won an Emmy award for his work in 1990.

Mary Eliza Church Terrell

Mary's father, a former slave, was perhaps the first African-American millionaire in the South, so the Churches ensured that their daughter received an outstanding education by sending her to Northern schools. In 1884, she earned her baccalaureate at Oberlin College, one of the first three African-American women to do so. Despite Oberlin's liberal reputation, Church still felt the sting of racism. Church became one of the first African-American women to receive a graduate degree, earning her master's degree (1888) from Oberlin. Three years later, she married Robert Terrell, a lawyer who later became the first African-American municipal-court judge in the District of Columbia.

In 1890, Terrell embarked on a 30-year public-speaking career. In her lectures and her writings, she advocated for women's rights, women's suffrage, African-American voting rights, civil rights, racial and civil justice, world peace, educational reform, and even kindergartens and child-care centers for the children of African-American working mothers. She also opposed lynching, racial segregation, racial discrimination in employment and schooling, unfair prosecution, and injustice and oppression in any form. Terrell received doctor of letters degrees from Oberlin, Wilberforce, and Howard Universities during the 1940s. A well-respected scholar, she fought for three years to force the American Association of University Women (AAUW) to accept her and other nonwhite women as members; she was admitted in 1949, when she was in her mid-eighties.

Terrell also participated actively in various polit-ical, social, and cultural organizations, and she was the first African-American woman appointed to a school board. Terrell also reached out globally, representing numerous American delegations at conventions in Germany, Switzerland, and England (addressing those gatherings in fluent German, French, and English). At ages 89 and 90, Terrell leaned on her cane as she led sit-ins, pickets, and boycotts to desegregate lunch counters and restaurants in our nation's capital. After a year of such actions, several department stores relented and desegregated their lunchrooms, but it took her lawsuit, culminating in a 1953 U.S. Supreme Court case, to desegregate the remaining eateries.

Lucy Terry
(married name: Prince)

In 1746, when she was about 16 years old, Terry wrote "Bars Fight," the first poem penned by a female African-American. "Bars Fight" wasn't actually published until 1855, so the first published poetry by an African-American was by Jupiter Hammon, and the first published poetry by an African-American woman was by Phillis Wheatley. The poem by Terry was not about a tavern brawl, but actually, the "Bars" to which she was referring was a patch of open meadow land by that name. The "Fight" she was describing was an engagement that resulted when some Native Americans (encouraged by French colonists) ambushed some English colonists.

Although she was born free in West Africa, she was just an infant when she was captured, too young to remember a time before her enslavement. She spent her first few years in Rhode Island, then at age 5, she was sold away to Massachusetts. In 1756, Justice of the Peace Ephraim Williams (later the founder of Williams College in Williamstown, Massachusetts) married her to Abijah Prince, from Curaçao, who was almost 25 years older than she. By the time they wedded, Prince was able to buy Lucy out of bondage and owned quite a bit of land. Their union proved fruitful, yielding six children, including one who later served in the Revolutionary War.

Theatre

In the decades before the Harlem Renaissance, when many Harlem theatres admitted only whites, the Lincoln Theatre's open-admissions policy made it the hot spot for Harlem's African-American audiences. On 135th Street at Lenox Avenue, the Lincoln catered to the community's working-class Southern immigrants. It was known for its live entertainment and lively audiences, who often participated in the onstage action with loud and witty running commentary. Pianist Thomas "Fats" Waller got his start at the Lincoln. So did "Mother of the Blues" Ma Rainey, "Empress of the Blues" Bessie Smith, jazz musician Duke Ellington and vaudeville entertainer Bert Williams.

The American Negro Theatre was a pioneering theater company and school in which several hundred African-American actors, writers, and technicians began their careers. The Academy Award-winning actor Sidney Poitier, the actor and singer Harry Belafonte, and the actress Ruby Dee are three of the prominent actors who were affiliated with the theatre. The American Negro Theater was founded in Harlem in 1940 by the black writer Abram Hill and the black actor Frederick O'Neal, who wanted to create a company that would provide opportunity for African-American artists and entertainment for African-American audiences that was unavailable downtown on Broadway.

The Black Theatre Alliance (BTA) was founded in 1971 in New York City to support the artistic and financial development of small commercially-owned African-American theater companies. Founded by playwrights Delano Stewart, Hazel Bryant, and Roger Furman, the Black Theatre Alliance initially was comprised of seven theater companies. The alliance provided technical equipment, graphics, funds, resources, information, and touring assistance. It compiled the Black Theatre Resources Directory, listing noncommercial black theater operations in the United States, theater technicians, administrators, artistic directors, and works by African-American playwrights. In 1972, the BTA began publishing a newsletter titled Black Theatre Alliance to encourage collaboration and to promote the activities of member theaters.

The Negro Ensemble Company was founded in New York City in 1967 by actor-director-playwright Douglas Turner Ward, actor Robert Hooks, and white manager Gerald Krone. Their intent was to provide a space where black playwrights could communicate with an audience of other African- Americans. The Negro Ensemble Company produced a very wide spectrum of plays, including family dramas, folk musicals, and plays from African and Caribbean perspectives.

Bessie Smith, "Empress of the Blues," in 1936.

Third World Press

Established in 1967, TWP is one of the oldest existing African-American publishing houses in the United States. It publishes fiction, history, essays, poetry, drama, and both young adult and children's literature that contributes to the positive development of people of African descent.

Thirteenth Amendment

The Thirteen amendment was the first of the Civil War amendments. Established in 1865, it prohibited slavery and guaranteed freedom for African-Americans. Nearly 4 million black slaves were freed.

The Capitol Building in Washington, D. C. during the debate over the Thirteen Amendment.

Clarence Thomas

When Thurgood Marshall retired in 1991, he was succeeded by another African-American associate justice, Clarence Thomas. The televised Senate committee hearings on the Thomas nomination received international notoriety in October 1991, when charges of sexual harassment were alleged against him by a former staff member, Anita Hill. The issue became controversial in itself, drawing attention to harassment in the workplace. Thomas was confirmed by a close vote in the full Senate, but the hearings had repercussions in the national elections of 1992.

Jean Toomer (né Nathan Pinchback Toomer)

During his lifetime, Toomer produced only one great work, the novel *Cane*. However, it was so brilliantly and artistically composed that it won Toomer great praise and renown as one of the most famous writers of the Harlem Renaissance. *Cane* has become part of the literary curriculum at many American schools.

Trickster tales

A trickster tale is a folktale in which the action of the story centers on a trickster character, and the fictional events in the story are intended to represent events in the real world. In most trickster tales, animal characters represent humans, speaking and behaving like humans, but occasionally, tricksters are actually humans-or even superhumans with some godlike characteristics. In all cases, trickster characters are wily, charming, and mischievous, and they almost invariably come into conflict with characters who are physically larger and more powerful than they, so they must use their craftiness to trick these more powerful adversaries.. As African slaves adapted to the American continent, they modified their tales to suit their new environs. They dropped animals native to Africa and incorporated animals of the American South. As Christianity became more widespread among African-Americans, tricksters lost their mythical powers. Increasingly, tricksters used sly cunning rather than supernatural powers to succeed. Further, these slaves, forbidden from gaining any formal education or even learning to read in a land where education connotes success, tell of tricksters who have masterful verbal skills and cunning wit. Prevented from open revolt, the African-American trickster uses artful subversion to undo the oppressor. Some stories, however, serve as cautionary tales, showing how the trickster's greed, gluttony, pride, or selfishness ends up harming the trickster at least as much as the object of the trickery. More contemporary trickster tales include Toni Morrison's *Tar Baby* (1981); Ishmael Reed's *The Last Days of Louisiana Red* (1974); Ralph Ellison's *Invisible Man* (1952), featuring con artist, gambler, and petty criminal Bliss Proteus Rinehart. Contemporary children's books featuring African or African-American trickster tales include Gerald McDermott's *Anansi the Spider* (1972) and his West African *Zomo the Rabbit* (1992); Ashley F. Bryan's *The Adventures of Aku* (1976) and

The Dancing Granny (1977), featuring "Ananse"; Louise Bennett's books about "Brer Anancy"; Eric Kimmel's Anansi and the Talking Melon (1994); and Julius Lester's The Last Tales of Uncle Remus: As Told by Julius Lester (1994).

William Trotter

The son of a Civil War veteran, successful real-estate broker, and author (about African-American achievements in music), young William attended mostly white schools, graduated magna cum laude from Harvard in 1895, and earned a master's degree a year later. He was the first African-American student at the university to be elected to Phi Beta Kappa. In 1901, at the age of 29, Trotter founded the Boston Guardian, a newspaper devoted to equal rights for African-Americans.

Sojourner Truth
(legal name: Isabella Van Wagenen; slave name: Isabella Baumfree or Bomefree)

Sojourner Truth was born into slavery in Hurley, Ulster County, New York. While still a child, Isabella was sold again and again. In 1827, the state of New York's Gradual Emancipation Act freed her. When Isabella was about 14 years old, another slave, Thomas, married her, and the twosome had five children. Even before Isabella's own emancipation she boldly resisted of slavery. A year before New York's emancipation law was enacted, she chose to leave her masters and went to work. Further, when her son was illegally sold into perpetual slavery in Alabama (just as New York state law was about to abolish slavery in New York), she solicited the aid of Ulster County Quakers and went to court to sue for his return-and won the suit! About that time, she also underwent a religious conversion. In 1843, she traveled the country, preaching the Christian gospel as she understood it. On June 1 of that year, she renamed herself "Sojourner Truth," thereby acknowledging her calling as an itinerant preacher. By the end of that year, Truth

Sojourner Truth was received by President Abraham Lincoln at the White House in 1964.

moved to a utopian community in Massachusetts, where she became a feminist abolitionist. There she met fellow abolitionists Frederick Douglass, David Ruggles, and William Lloyd Garrison. Truth dictated a slave narrative to a neighbor, Olive Gilbert. The Boston printer of Garrison's Liberator newspaper printed it as The Narrative of Sojourner Truth: A Bondswoman of Olden Time (1850). Truth sold copies for 25¢ apiece to listeners at her sermons and speeches. A powerful orator, in 1851, Truth gave perhaps one of the most famous speeches in American history to the Ohio Women's Rights Convention: "And A'n't I a Woman?" In that speech, she cited numerous ways in which African-American and working-class women had worked hard and had suffered much, thereby showing that many women are neither fragile nor protected from hardship. This speech (printed on June 21, 1851, in the Anti-Slavery Bugle) and a contact with Harriet Beecher Stowe (author of the 1852 book Uncle Tom's Cabin) helped publicize Truth and her book. During the Civil War, Truth helped supply food and clothing to African-

American Union soldiers, and she fervently encouraged other African-Americans to join that army. On October 29, 1864, President Abraham Lincoln received her at the White House. During the post-Civil War period, Truth worked tirelessly to aid former slaves and war refugees in gaining employment and job skills.

Harriet Tubman
(née Araminta Ross)
renamed Harriet by her mother

In her 20 or so trips, Tubman never lost a single Underground Railroad passenger. By the time Civil War was declared, slavehunters and slaveholders had

Harriet Tubman guided slaves to freedom in the Underground Railroad.

posted a $40,000 price tag on her head. Born a slave, she escaped to freedom in 1849. But she did not seek safety and security for herself. Instead, for a decade or more, she led about 300 people out of bondage-including her parents and several other relatives. Although she never learned to read or write, her speeches rallied support for abolition and motivated listeners to contribute time and money, and she even inspired some to put their own lives on the line just as she did, conducting and safe-housing fugitives on the Underground. "Wade in the Water" and several other Negro spirituals are attributed to her. During the Civil War, she worked for the Union Army, spying, scouting, nursing, and cooking close to the action. She even led a Union raid, which freed 750 enslaved African-Americans, and served at the Battle of Fort Wagner, at which the 54th Massachusetts Colored Regiment fought valiantly. About three decades later, in 1896, Tubman bought 25 acres of land adjacent to her house, a former way station on the Underground Railroad. There, she built The Harriet Tubman House for Aged and Indigent Colored People. She herself moved into that home in about 1911. On her death, she was given a burial with full military honors, in recognition of her service to the Union Army. Both her funeral and her headstone were paid for by the National Association of Colored Women.

Lorenzo Dow Turner

Turner's *Africanisms in Gullah Dialect* (1949) was instrumental in revealing how much of African languages have been preserved in the speech of African-Americans. For example, there's *danshiki* (Yoruba), from which we have the dashiki; *dzug* (meaning "misbehave" in Wolof), which led to our juke joints; *mbanzo* (Kimdunu), our banjo; and *jaja* and *nyambi* (Bantu) gave us our jazz and yam. Turner also turned out numerous articles and essays on linguistics, as well as his doctoral dissertation (Anti-Slavery Sentiment in American Literature Prior to 1865), and he wrote two more books, based on his proverb- and folktale-gathering sojourn to West Africa.

Nat Turner

We know him chiefly through his "Confessions." Although Turner had learned to read and write at an early age–unusual for a boy raised in slavery–he dictated it to his white confessor, Thomas Ruffin Gray, Turner's court-appointed attorney and unsympathetic scribe. For three days, Gray (who offered no defense of Turner in court) recorded Turner's story.

In Turner's eyes, God had specially chosen him to be His instrument of vengeance and of violent insurrection against white oppressors who were holding fellow blacks in bondage. Born a slave himself, Turner was a deeply religious child and youth. He believed that God had revealed to him his mission through divine visions: The first, in 1825, showed him "white spirits and black spirits engaged in battle, and the sun darkened-the thunder rolled in the heavens, and blood flowed in streams." His second vision, May 12, 1828, gave him his messianic assignment to lead his slave rebellion: "I heard a loud noise in the heavens, and the Spirit instantly appeared to me and said . . . Christ had laid down the yoke he had borne for the sins of men, and that I should take it on and fight ... And by the signs in the heavens that it would make known to me when I should commence the great work, and until the first sign appeared I should conceal it from the knowledge of men."

When, in February of 1831, Turner saw a solar eclipse, he believed it to be the sign he awaited. On August 21, he and his followers (said to number 70 or 80 at the peak of the revolt) began a 40-hour rampage, killing 57 white men, women (starting with the widow of his former owner), and children. Turner had envisioned that once the whites were terrified into seeing the error of their cruel enslavement of blacks, the whites would surrender, and the bloodshed could stop.

This part of Turner's vision was definitely not to come to pass. A white militia had been called to arms, which killed many of the rebels outright, caught and hanged others of them, and scattered the rest, and Turner went into hiding, but was captured, jailed, and convicted. He was hanged on November 11. Following the rebellion, blacks-enslaved or not-were targets for every malicious white brute in the South, and any Southern whites who may have been sympathetic to abolition were either turned around or silenced. The crime of teaching an African-American to read drew much harsher penalties, African-American preachers had to go underground and avoid public notice, and the Bible was barred from being held by black hands.

Tuskegee Airmen

Beginning in Tuskegee, Alabama in 1941 at the Tuskegee Army Airfield, the Tuskegee Airmen were formed and trained by the U.S. Army Air Corps. During a period when racial discrimination overshadowed the country, approximately 1,000 airmen were trained and about 445 went overseas during World War II. They were eventually honored with over 150 Distinguished Flying Cross awards. Known as the black fighter pilots of the 99th Pursuit Squadron, later incorporated into the 332nd Fighter Group, the airmen were responsible for escorting bomber planes that flew over Asia and Europe during May 1942 and June 9, 1945. They were the only unit never to lose one bomber, although they did lose 66 men, 32 of whom fell into enemy hands. The Tuskegee Airmen are also credited as being the first American flyers to cause a German destroyer to sink. In total they shot down hundreds of enemy aircraft.

Tuskegee University

In February 1881, the Alabama legislature voted to set aside $2,000 each year to fund a state and normal school for blacks in Tuskegee. The trustees asked officials at several other black institutions to recommend someone to head the new school. Although they were suggesting white candidates, Hampton Institute's president Samuel Chapman Armstrong recommended his black protégé, Booker T. Washington. On July 4, Washington opened the Normal School for colored teachers at Tuskegee in a shack next to a black Methodist church. The first 30 students ranged in age from 16 to 40. Most were teachers hoping to further their own education. Washington held a fervent belief that industrial education and training was the key to success for African-Americans. Students were required to learn a trade and perform manual labor at the school, including making and laying the bricks for the buildings that became the first campus.

Tuskegee's charter had mandated that tuition would be free for students who committed to teaching in Alabama public schools. The students' labor helped with financial costs, and Washington solicited much of the remaining funding from northern white philan-thropists. Tuskegee was incorporated as a private institution in 1892, and its name was changed to the Tuskegee Normal and Industrial Institute that year. Social norms prohibited white instructors from serving under a black principal, so Tuskegee became the first institution of higher learning with a black faculty. In 1896 the school hired George Washington Carver, whose groundbreaking agricultural research received international recognition. After Booker T. Washington's death in 1915, the industrial training approach changed and Tuskegee awarded its first bachelor's degree in 1925. Its first college curriculum began in 1927 and graduate programs were eventually added. In the 1960s and 1970s Tuskegee became the first black college to be designated a Registered National Historic Landmark and a National Historic Site. By the school's centennial in 1981, Tuskegee's campus included 150 buildings on 5,000 acres, and its endowment was approximately $22 million. Today, approximately 3,200 undergraduates are enrolled at Tuskegee, and there are an additional 200 graduate students.

A class at Tuskegee Institute.

Underground Railroad

The Underground Railroad was the informal network of travel routes and intermittent rest stations used by slaves who were making their escape to freedom in Canada or other safe areas in the states. The railroad was loosely organized and operated with the help of individual people who were sympathetic to the slaves. There were no specific conductors or stations and it was neither underground nor a railroad. The system was a loose network of aid and assistance to slaves fleeing from bondage. It is estimated that as many as one hundred thousand enslaved persons may have escaped in the years between the American Revolution and the Civil War. The most heavily traveled routes of the Underground Railroad went through Ohio, Indiana, and western Pennsylvania. Large numbers of fugitives followed these routes and arrived in Canada by way of Detroit or Niagara Falls, New York. Some slaves sailed across Lake Erie to Ontario from ports in Erie, Pennsylvania, and Sandusky, Ohio. In the East, the main center of the Underground Railroad was southeastern Pennsylvania. Many slaves followed routes from there through New England to Quebec. Levi Coffin, a Quaker who lived in Newport Indiana, helped over 3,000 slaves find freedom. His home was on three of the major routes. Harriet

Tubman is heralded as the African-American whose courageous efforts helped hundreds of slaves escape to freedom. She became the most famous leader of the Underground Railroad.

United Negro College Fund, Inc.

Spearheaded in 1943 by Dr. Frederick D. Patterson, President of Tuskegee Institute, the United Negro College Fund, Inc. was incorporated on April 25, 1944 with 27 member colleges. Dr. Patterson's idea to pool the monies of black private colleges grew to become one of the country's oldest and most prosperous organizations, raising $1.6 billion in its 56 years. The fund provides financial assistance to deserving minority students for their higher education. The organization strives to raise the quality of education by supporting the operations of member colleges and universities and by providing financial assistance to member institutions. The fund also strives to increase access to technology for students and faculty at member schools. UNCF recently started a partnership with Microsoft, IBM, and AT&T. Presently, the UNCF membership includes 41 four-year private historically black colleges and universities. The Non-Profit Times and The Chronicle of Philanthropy rank UNCF among the top 100 charitable organizations in the country.

George B. (Boyer) Vashon

In 1838, 14-year-old George was secretary of the first Junior Anti-Slavery Society in America, and in

1844, he made history as the first African-American to graduate from Oberlin College. He then studied to become an attorney in Pittsburgh, Pennsylvania, but his race barred him from admission to the state bar. After a 30-month sojourn to Haiti, he returned to the States and was admitted to the New York bar in 1848, the first African-American to do so in that state.

Carl Van Vechten

Carl Van Vechten, of European-American ancestry, spent much of his life championing the literature and culture of African-Americans. Among other things, he collected African-American literary works and founded the James Weldon Johnson Memorial Collection of Negro Arts and Letters (housed at Yale University), the Carl Van Vechten Collection at the New York City Public Library, and the George Gershwin Memorial Collection of Music and Musical Literature at Fisk University in Nashville, Tennessee. Van Vechten was the most prominent European American associated with the Harlem Renaissance in New York, where he hosted a literary salon and advanced the writings of Langston Hughes, Helene Johnson, James Weldon Johnson, Nella Larsen, and other writers of that era.. His most acclaimed novel was written about these experiences and was intended to showcase the riches of African-American culture, but his choice of title, *Nigger Heaven* (1926), divided the African-American literary community.

Denmark Vesey's 1812 Conspiracy

African born Denmark Vesey was a seaman and a former slave. He was very intelligent and spoke many languages. Vesey found himself in a position to buy his own freedom. As a freeman, he made a plan to bring about the downfall of the city of Charleston on July 14, 1812. His plan failed, and he was hanged on July 2nd for an insurrection that never took place.

Vietnam War

For the first time in its history, America entered a war with racially integrated armed forces. Despite the military's overall success with racial integration, there were still striking imbalances in the Vietnam era. During 1965-1967, the black casualty rate of 20 percent was roughly twice that of whites. During 1967, 64 percent of eligible blacks were drafted, compared with only 31 percent of whites. Blacks were less likely to meet the higher educational requirements of the navy and air force. Thus, they overwhelmingly entered the army. They were also underrepresented in the officer corps. In 1968 blacks made up nearly 10 percent of total American military personnel, but only 2 percent of all officers.

African Americans showed their bravery quickly in Vietnam. Two of the war's earliest Congressional Medal of Honor recipients, Private Milton Olive and medic Lawrence Joel, were African Americans. Black servicemen in Vietnam referred to themselves as "bloods." Yet Vietnam remained a place of much interracial cooperation. Combat troops realized that they had to count on one another regardless of race. They fought a bitter jungle war in which there were no decisive engagements and the threat of ambush and booby traps was ever present. Vietnam's dangers also included drug dependency. Many soldiers, white and black, suffered devastating personal consequences.

Alice Walker

Alice Walker's poems, essays, short stories and novels are honest, direct, open writings that use her own and others' experiences as material for her searing examination of politics and black-white relations. In her first novel, *The Third Life of Grange Copeland* (1970), Walker told of how three generations of one family were affected by their move from the South to the North. Her first collection of stories was *In Love and Trouble* (1973) and her novel *Meridian* was published in 1976.

Perhaps her most famous work is *The Color Purple* (1982), for which Walker won the American Book Award and the Pulitzer Prize. She was the first African-American woman to win the latter. *The Color Purple* captured the attention of mainstream America through the film adaptation by Steven Spielberg. Walker refuses to ignore the tangle of personal and political themes in her novels, which also include *Temple of My Familiar* (1989), and *Possessing the Secret of Joy* (1992). She also has a collection of short stories, *You Can't Keep a Good Woman Down* (1979) and has written volumes of poetry and essays. Walker is an activist for women's rights, and she helped bring Zora Neale Hurston back to literary eminence. In 1979 Walker edited an anthology of Hurston's writing, *I Love Myself When I'm Laughin.*

David Walker

After publishing his pamphlet, "David Walker's Appeal in Four Articles; Together With a Preamble, to the Coloured Citizens of the World, but in Particular, and Very Expressly, to Those of the United States of America," a reward was offered for his capture: $1,000 if caught dead, and $10,000 if captured alive. Walkder recited the atrocities of slavery and urged slaves to revolt. Walker scathingly rebuked all those who participated in perpetuating slavery, and predicted that slave traders, slaveholders, and blacks and whites who didn't actively fight against them would suffer the wrath of God. Walker was also a believer in the subversive power of education. Restrictions against letting slaves learn to read and write were tightened after Walker's pamphlet was published. Self-educated and born free, Walker self-published his Appeal (although an earlier, briefer version had appeared in *Freedom's Journal*, to which he was a frequent contributor). Despite the banning of its circulation by several state legislatures (including Georgia's) and other energetic attempts to block its distribution,

it managed to circulate. By early 1830, Walker released his third edition of his Appeal. By the end of that year, Walker was found dead, probably murdered by poisoning. In 1848, Henry Highland Garnet reprinted it, along with his own provocative "*Address to the Slaves of the United States.*"

Wyatt Tee Walker

Wyatt Tee Walker became the executive director of the Southern Christian Leadership Conference in 1960. He authored protest strategies that included the Birmingham campaign of April 1963. Walker left the SCLC in 1964, settled in New York City, and continued to work for social justice. He also wrote gospel music. He has been the pastor of Canaan Baptist Church of Christ in Harlem since 1967.

Booker T. Washington

From 1895 until his death in 1915, Booker Taliferro Washington, an ex-slave who had built Tuskegee Institute in Alabama into a major center of industrial training for black youths, was the nation's dominant black leader. Washington was an African-American

educator and orator born to a slave in Franklin County, Virginia in 1856. After overcoming humble roots as a salt furnace worker and coal miner, he began attending the Hampton Institute in 1879. Washington called on both blacks and whites to come together. He urged whites to employ the masses of black laborers. He called on blacks to cease agitating for political and social rights and to concentrate instead on working to improve their economic conditions. Washington felt that excessive stress had been placed on liberal arts education for blacks. He believed that their need to earn a living called instead for training in crafts and trades. Washington held to

Booker T. Washington believed that all blacks should receive some industrial training as well as academics.

the belief that Blacks could rise to self-respect and economic independence through education and skill development. In an effort to spur the growth of black business enterprise, Washington also organized the National Negro Business League in 1900. But African-American businessmen were handicapped by insufficient capital and by the competition of white-owned big businesses. Washington's influence became more widespread when he became an instructor at the Hampton Institute where he originated night school. He became a leading African-American educator and was chosen to create a normal and industrial school in Tuskeegee, Alabama in 1881. Despite personal and family tragedies, he managed to build his institute for African-American education in the hostile territory of the post-Reconstruction South. The programs emphasized industrial training for African-Americans.

He opposed the Northward emigration of Southern blacks and quietly complied with segregation. Washington was highly successful in winning influential white support. The more praise whites heaped upon him, the more scorn blacks piled on. He soon had virulently outspoken opponents among civil-rights activists such as W. E. B. Du Bois. Nonetheless, Washington became the most powerful black man in the nation's history. He dined at the White House, was consulted by Presidents Theodore Roosevelt and William Howard Taft, and was respected as the African-American expert on race matters. His good deeds to his supporters were numerous. But his program of vocational training did not meet the changing needs of industry, and the harsh reality of discrimination prevented most of his Tuskegee Institute graduates from using their skills. When Washington died, 34 years after he had opened the school (with 1 teacher, 2 ramshackle buildings, and 50 students), the Tuskegee Institute had a faculty of nearly 200 instructors, more than 100 well-equipped buildings, and an endowment of about $2 million.

Walter E. Washington

Washington was the first black chief executive of a major city. He was an appointee who became the commissioner of Washington, D.C., in 1967.

Robert C. (Clifton) Weaver

Weaver's explorations in the fields of sociology and economics include nearly 200 articles and 4 books: *Negro Labor: A National Problem* (1946), *The Negro Ghetto* (1948), *The Urban Complex* (1964), and *Dilemmas of Urban America* (1965). These works (and his involvement in several governmental positions) contributed to his becoming the first African-American appointed to the U.S. Cabinet, as the Secretary of Housing and Urban Development from 1966 to 1968.

Ida B. (Bell) Wells (-Barnett) (née Wells)

While a student at Fisk University in 1853, Wells started writing for the student newspaper, and soon started writing for numerous African-American newspapers on various topics. Among her many topics was an experience that heralded Rosa Parks's stand against segregated bus transportation in 1955. In 1884, Wells had paid for a first-class ladies coach ticket on a train, but she was physically removed from that car and dragged to the smoking car, where all "colored" people were ordered to ride. She sued the Chesapeake, Ohio, and Southwestern Railroad and won a $500 settlement in a Tennessee circuit court. (Unfortunately, she later lost when the railroad appealed to the Tennessee Supreme Court, which overturned the lower-court decision.) Another of her favorite topics was the inferiority of segregated schools for African-American children. As a teacher (and a former student of segregated schools), she knew her subject firsthand. Although she wrote all her newspaper articles under the pseudonym "Iola," the Memphis school board eventually realized she had authored these critical articles, and in 1891, the board refused to renew her teaching contract.

Wells turned her attention to journalism full time. She wrote scathing editorials denouncing lynching as a brutal means of squelching economic competition from African Americans—not, as was often claimed, an overly enthusiastic defense of white women's virtue against black men's sexual aggression. She urged the African-Americans of Memphis to flee from lynching and Jim Crow racism, and to go West to find genuine economic and social opportunity. Memphis whites destroyed her newspaper's offices and loudly warned Wells never to return to Memphis—under penalty of death. She stayed clear of Memphis, but she did not stop speaking out against lynching and other aspects of racism. She published her 1892 pamphlet, "Southern Horrors: Lynch Law in All Its Phases."

Occasionally, Wells attacked problems of northern racism. In 1893, when African-Americans were barely included in the exhibition of the Chicago World's Fair, Wells asked Frederick Douglass, Chicago attorney and newspaper publisher Ferdinand Lee Barnett, and other prominent African-Americans to help her publish 20,000 copies of her pamphlet "The Reason Why the Colored American Is Not in the World's Columbian Exposition." Wells also joined with others in support of racial and gender equality. In addition to joining many organizations, she founded or co-founded the Ida B. Wells Club of Chicago (1893); the National Association of Colored Women (1896); the Niagara Movement (1905) and its successor, the NAACP (1910); the Negro Fellowship League (1910); and the Alpha Suffrage Club of Chicago (1913). In 1930, she rejected her Republican Party affiliation and ran as an independent candidate for the Illinois senate, but she lost her bid. Sixty years later, however, she won a place on a U.S. postage stamp, the first African-American woman journalist to be so honored.

Cornel West

Teacher, philosopher, writer, theologian, sociologist, some say that West is the first leading African-American intellectual to rise to prominence since W. E. B. Du Bois in the late nineteenth and early twentieth centuries. In 1988, West led Princeton's Afro-American Studies program. In 1994, he went to Harvard University with dual teaching appointments (in the School of Divinity and in the Faculty of Arts and Sciences). West and his Harvard colleague William Julius Wilson simultaneously became full professors in 1995, the first African-Americans to achieve the highest academic post possible at that university.

His body of work includes: *Prophesy Deliverance!: An Afro-American Revolutionary Christianity* (1982), *Prophetic Fragments*, 1988; *The Ethical Dimensions of Marxist Thought*, 1991; *Breaking Bread: Insurgent Black Intellectual Life*, 1991; *Prophetic Reflections: Notes on*

Race and Power in America, 1993; *Race Matters*, 1993; and *Keeping Faith: Philosophy and Race in America*, 1993. He also co-authored *Jews and Blacks: Let the Healing Begin*, 1995, *The Future of the Race*, 1996, and *The War Against Parents: What We Can Do for America's Beleaguered Moms and Dads*, 1998, co-author.

Race Matters became a bestseller and is the book that earned West the most notoriety and it is the most accessible to the general public, leading some to call him a "public intellectual."

Phillis Wheatley

One of the earliest known African-American writers and the first to publish a book of poetry was former slave Phillis Wheatley. Wheatley was "purchased" by John and Susanna Wheatley in 1761 Boston. Although Wheatley is believed to have been born in West Africa. She was tutored by the Wheatleys' daughter and perhaps others, and Phillis attained a level of education that even most white females did not enjoy at that time. Wheatley's education was rooted in literary classics. Wheatley and her poetry thus compose what was considered to be an odd combination-a black female slave with much education and low social status who wrote critically acclaimed poetry. This combination of factors was so unusual that when Wheatley's book, Poems on Various Subjects, Religious and Moral by Phillis Wheatley, Negro Servant to Mr. John Wheatley, of Boston, in New England, was released in London in 1773, it included statements that testified to the authenticity of Wheatley and her 38 poems. One statement included the signatures of 18 well-respected Boston men, such as the governor of Massachusetts and John Hancock. Wheatley sailed to England in the

spring of 1773 to participate in the publication of her book. While in London, Wheatley toured the city as a free human being, giving readings of her poetry and meeting Benjamin Franklin and other noted personalities. Wheatley had been previously published in New England area newspapers, and she continued to write for several more years after the publication of her book. She also wrote a letter and poem to George Washington in 1776, which so impressed him that Wheatley gained an audience with him during the Revolutionary War.

Bill White

White became the first African-American to head a major professional sports organization when he was named president of baseball's National League in 1989.

Douglas Wilder

Douglas Wilder was born in Richmond Virginia on January 17, 1931. He graduated Virginia Union University in 1951 from Howard University Law School in 1959. He had a lucrative career in law and real estate until 1969. Then in 1970 he was elected to the Virginia legislature and became the first African-American to hold state-wide office since the Reconstruction. As a 16-year member of the state senate he was an advocate for fair housing legislation, labor-union rights for government employees and an increase in minority hiring. In 1985 he was elected lieutenant governor of Virginia and in 1989 Wilder became the country's first elected black governor (in the same state where his grandparents were once slaves). His fiscally conservative politics drew national attention and did not boost his following. In 1994 he left office.

Roy Wilkins

Born in St. Louis, Missouri in 1901, Roy Wilkins worked alongside Dr. Martin Luther King, Jr. and other leaders throughout the Civil Rights Movement. Made assistant executive secretary for the National Association of Colored People (NAACP) in 1931, he was editor of the NAACP's official magazine, The Crisis, from 1934 until 1949. Wilkins played an major role in winning the historic 1954 Supreme Court decision that overturned the doctrine of "separate but equal" educational facilities, and helped to organize the 1963 March on Washington. Wilkins became the NAACP executive director in 1965. Militants tried to force his resignation because he rejected black separatism, but he continued to serve until 1977.

Bert Williams

Of mixed black and white ancestry, Williams used standard blackface makeup and disguised his voice to portray the shuffling, drawling stereotype popularized by minstrel shows. Williams formed a vaudeville team with George Walker in 1895. He appeared in the all-black musical In Dahomey on Broadway and in London in 1903. He was the leading comedian in the Ziegfeld Follies 1910-17. Williams composed his own songs, including "Woodman, Spare that Tree" and the wry "Nobody."

Daniel Hale Williams

Dr. Daniel Hale Williams was an African-American born in 1856 who went on to become a doctor and the founder of Provident Hospital and Training School on May 4, 1891. He is acknowledged as being the first doctor to carry out open-heart surgery with success on July 9, 1893. Williams died in 1931.

George Washington Williams

Williams, generally recognized as the first major African-American historian, wrote History of the Negro Race in America from 1619 to 1880 (1883), considered the first fully encompassing history of African-Americans up to that time.

Peter Williams, Jr.

In 1827, Williams helped found Freedom's Journal, an ardently abolitionist newspaper. Williams, the first African-American Episcopalian priest, was active in the American Anti-Slavery Society until rumors that he had celebrated an interracial marriage abruptly ended his leadership role. He continued his church service.

August (né Frederick August Kittel) Wilson

Inspired by the Black Aesthetic movement, Wilson has written several historic plays.

His first commercial success was Ma Rainey's Black Bottom (1984). Ma Rainey is set in 1927 Chicago in a backstage room for a celebrated blues singer who verbally abuses the musicians who accompany her. The Broadway production of Fences earned Wilson the 1987 Pulitzer Prize for drama, in addition to Tony Awards for best play, best director, best actor, and best featured actress. Following *Fences*, the *Chicago Tribune* also named Wilson its Artist of the Year. In addition to achieving great critical success, the play grossed a record-breaking $11 million in one year, more than any other nonmusical play at that time. The 1990 Broadway production of Wilson's *The Piano Lesson* earned Wilson a second Pulitzer Prize for drama (1990), as well as an additional Tony Award for best play.

Wilson has also been elected to the American Academy of Arts and Sciences (1991), and he was one of 10 writers to win the generous Whiting Writer's Awards in recognition of his "exceptionally promising, emerging talent." In 1988, Wilson also received an honorary degree from Yale University, the home of the repertory theater where most of his plays have been produced.

Harriet E. (née Adams) Wilson

For generations, literary scholars who had come across her novel, *Our Nig; or, Sketches from the Life of a Free Black, in a Two-Story White House, North. Showing That Slavery's Shadows Fall Even There* (1859), had believed that the author was white, perhaps even male. In 1984, Henry Louis Gates, Jr. affirmed that Wilson was a black woman, the first African-American to publish a novel in the United States.

Wilson created her own unique literary contribution, drawing on the techniques of her white female contemporaries when it suited her tale, and borrowing the techniques of slave narrators when it fit her purpose. She broke new ground by realistically examining the life experiences of an ordinary African-American woman.

Historians and other scholars have been able to find out very little about Harriet Wilson before 1850, when she was in her early twenties. What is known about her after that time is based on her autobiographical novel. On October 6, 1851, Harriet married Thomas Wilson, a beguiling abolitionist lecturer who passed himself off as a Virginia-born fugitive slave reporting the horrors of his slave experiences, but who was actually a freeman. After Harriet became pregnant, Thomas abandoned her and went to sea. In late May or early June of 1852, Harriet gave birth to a son, George Mason Wilson. After George's birth, Thomas

returned from the sea, retrieved his wife and child, and supported them fairly well for a while. After a bit, however, he left again, never to return, and Harriet had to place George in the care of kindly white foster parents in New Hampshire while she tried to improve her health and to make enough money to retrieve him. She turned to writing, hoping to make enough to support herself and to retrieve George by writing a novel.

Wilson's protagonist, Alfrado ("Frado"), is modeled after herself. At the end of the novel, Frado and her infant are homeless and desperately impoverished. Her novel's ending certainly deviates from the typical ending of sentimental novels, in which the heroine is happily wedded at the conclusion of the book. Wilson closes her book with a direct appeal to her readers to help her gain enough money to retrieve her son from foster care.

Wilson finished writing her novel in 1859, and on August 18, she registered its copyright in the district of Massachusetts. On September 5, she paid to have the book published by an obscure Boston printer. She was the first African-American woman to publish a book of any kind in English, and the fifth African-American to publish a book of fiction in English. Tragically, Wilson's son died before she could earn enough to retrieve him. The location and date of Wilson's death are not now known.

Oprah (Gail) Winfrey

In 1984, Oprah Winfrey hosted a half-hour television talk show, *A.M. Chicago*, which aired against the highly popular national talk-show host Phil Donahue; no previous hosts had been able to touch Donahue in the ratings. Within a month, however, Oprah's ratings were equaling Donahue's. In 1985, the expanded hour-long show was renamed *The Oprah Winfrey Show*, and Donahue moved his show from Chicago to New York. In 1986, Oprah's show was syndicated, and over time, she reached top national ratings. In 1997, Oprah was still reaching about 15-20 million U.S. TV viewers every day, in addition to numerous other viewers in more than 130 other countries. The show has earned Winfrey six Emmy awards for best host, as well as 19 other Emmys. Winfrey's other awards include having been named one of the

25 most influential people in the world by *Time* magazine (1996) and the Woman of Achievement Award from the National Organization for Women (1986). She has also earned the highly esteemed Peabody Award (both for her talk show and for her charitable work), and the NAACP's Image Award four years in a row (1989-1992).

Winfrey owns her own production company, Harpo ("Oprah" spelled backwards), and has assets sometimes estimated at $250 million. In addition to funding scholarships, Winfrey finances countless charitable and philanthropic endeavors.

Harpo Productions also has enabled Winfrey to produce television and film projects she believes in, such as the 1988 miniseries *The Women of Brewster Place* (based on Gloria Naylor's novel), the television movie *The Wedding* (based on Dorothy West's novel), and the 1998 film *Beloved* (based on Toni Morrison's novel. In addition to her roles in *Brewster Place* and in *Beloved*, Winfrey gave an Oscar-nominated performance in Alice Walker's *The Color Purple* (1985).

Oprah has done much to promote the works of individual women writers, as well as reading through "Oprah's Book Club," launched in 1996, which has highlighted such books as the *Norton Anthology of African-American Literature*. Through her club, she announces in advance particular books to read, and then discusses these books with viewers on subsequent shows. A profile on Oprah's Book Club essentially ensures that a book will become a bestseller. She has been also involved with several book projects of her own including *Oprah: An Autobiography*, *In the Kitchen with Rosie: Oprah's Favorite Recipes*, and *The Uncommon Wisdom of Oprah Winfrey*.

Tiger Woods

Tiger Woods began playing golf as soon as he could walk, and by the age of three was shooting a 48 for nine holes. At 15, he became the youngest player ever to win the United States Golf Association (USGA) Junior National Championship, and in 1992, while at Stanford University, he won it for the third consecutive time. He captured several amateur championships and in 1996 turned pro. When he won the Masters Championship in 1997, Woods became the first African-American to win a major golf tournament. In 1997 he earned the PGA Player of the Year Award and was named Male Athlete of the Year by the Associated Press. He continues to have an outstanding record in professional golf.

Carter G. (Godwin) Woodson

Called the "Father of Black History," Woodson cofounded the Association for the Study of Negro (renamed Afro-American) Life and History in Washington, D.C. in 1915, with the aim of collecting sociological and historical data on the Negro, to study of peoples of African blood. Woodson helped to unearth the unspoken contributions of African-Americans to their country of birth, to probe the hidden lives of African-Americans, and to unveil the secrets of African-American culture and lift up the glories of the African past. Natural outgrowths of the organization were two journals: *The Journal of Negro History* (starting in 1916) was aimed at scholars, and the *Negro History Bulletin* (starting in 1937) was intended to aid schoolteachers from the primary grades through high school. The ASNLH's Associated Publishers was established in 1920 to put out publications on African-American history that would otherwise never reach their increasingly numerous readers.

Woodson's own works in this field were many. For decades, his *The Negro in Our History* (1922; 1962) was the primary textbook on African-American history, used chiefly in colleges, but also in high schools. In *The Mis-Education of the Negro* (1933) he saw the lack of education of African-Americans as a tragic waste of potential, and he urged readers to focus on developing the most precious resource of the African-American community: the minds of black people. He pointed out the absence of African-Americans in textbooks and in the curricula, starting in the primary grades and continuing through college and even into graduate schools. He repudiated the self-loathing that a flawed education can cause. One of the ways in which Woodson attempted to correct the educational failures he saw was by initiating Negro History Week in 1926. Initially set for the second week in February, embracing the birthdays of Frederick Douglass and

Abraham Lincoln, the celebration has since expanded to make all of February Black History Month.

World War I

When the United States entered World War I in April 1917, most African-Americans supported the move. During the war, about 1,400 black officers were commissioned. Some 200,000 blacks served abroad, though most were restricted to labor battalions and service regiments. Some blacks opposed involvement in World War I. Black Socialists A. Philip Randolph and Chandler Owen argued that the fight for democracy at home should precede the fight for it abroad.

World War II

The industrial boom that began with the outbreak of World War II in Europe in 1939 ended the depression. However, unemployed whites were generally the first to be given jobs. Discrimination against blacks in hiring impelled A. Philip Randolph, head of the Brotherhood of Sleeping Car Porters, to threaten a mass protest march on Washington. To forestall the march, scheduled for June 25, 1941, President Roosevelt issued Executive Order 8802 banning "discrimination in the employment of workers in defense industries or government" and establishing a Fair Employment Practices Committee (FEPC) to investigate violations. Although discrimination remained widespread, during the war blacks secured more jobs at better wages in a greater range of occupations than ever before. In World War II, as in World War I, there was a mass migration of blacks from the rural South. Some 1.5 million blacks left the South during the 1940s, mainly for the industrial cities of the North. Once again, serious housing shortages and job competition led to increased racial tension. Race riots broke out, the worst in Detroit in June 1943.

During the war, which the United States had entered in December 1941, a large proportion of black soldiers overseas were in service units, and combat troops remained segregated. In the course of the war, however, the Army introduced integrated officer training, and Benjamin O. Davis, Sr., became its first black brigadier general. In 1949, four years after the end of World War II, the armed services finally adopted a policy of integration.

Richard (Nathaniel) Wright

Portrait of Richard Wright, 1939.

Wright's novel Native Son and his autobiography Black Bo: A Record of Childhood and Youth (1945) are often required reading in high schools and colleges throughout the U.S. James Baldwin, Ralph Ellison and numerous other important writers have credited Wright with blazing the trail for fellow African-American novelists to follow. In 1941 he also wrote a pictorial history of blacks in America, 12 Million Black Voices: A Folk History of the American Negro. Wright was targeted by Senator Eugene McCarthy's red-baiting witch hunts, searching for "dangerous communists". Even though Wright had pointedly resigned from the Communist Party in the early 1940s, he was still subject to CIA and FBI surveillance, even while he lived in France. He became involved with poets and novelists of the Négritude movement, including Leopold Senghor and Aime Cesaire, with whom he founded Présence Africaine. During his Parisian exile, Wright wrote three more novels, a collection of lectures, a conference report, and two other works of nonfiction. Following his death, several of his works have been published. In 1961, a collection of short stories he had written previously, *Eight Men*, was published. Each story presents a different slant on how black men struggle to survive in the racial hatred of white-dominated America. In 1963, a novel he had written in the mid-1930s, *Lawd Today!* was published. Early in his career, Wright had written poetry, and during his final illness, the majority of his writing again turned to poems. About two years before he died, Wright proceeded to write more than 4,000 haiku poems.

York

York was an athletic black slave who was owned by Clark of Lewis and Clarke who made the historic expedition through the west from Missouri to Oregon in 1804. It is believed that York was the first black man ever seen by Native Americans in his time.

Andrew Young

A disciple of civil rights leader Martin Luther King, Jr., Andrew Young helped to draft the Civil Rights Act of 1964 and the Voting Rights Act of 1965. In 1972 Young was he was elected to Congress as a representative of Georgia, the first black congressman from the South since the post-Civil War Reconstruction Era. From there he was appointed U.S. Ambassador to the United Nations by President Jimmy Carter, but later resigned because of conflicts caused by his contacts with the Palestine Liberation Organization. In 1992 Young was elected mayor of Atlanta and served eight years.

Whitney Young

Born in 1921 at the Lincoln Institute, a private high school for blacks in Kentucky where his father was the first black principal, Whitney Young started out with a career in education. After serving as the dean of the school of social work at Atlanta University, Young became director of the National Urban League in 1961. He served until 1971 during one of the most turbulent times in civil rights history. His work with the National Urban League focused on gaining greater opportunities for blacks, especially in business and politics. During the Kennedy and Johnson administrations, he also became part of seven presidential commissions, and in 1969 he was awarded the Presidential Medal of Freedom.

Zawadi

The *Zawadi* are the gifts that are shared during Kwanzaa. Family members are rewarded with *Zawadi* for the obligations and quests they have accomplished.

INDEX